BIGGER

BIGGER

GOD'S REBUILDING PROCESS

THE WORKBOOK STUDY OF NEHEMIAH

KRISTAN DOOLEY

New York

BIGGER

GOD'S REBUILDING PROCESS

THE WORKBOOK STUDY OF NEHEMIAH

Published in New York, New York, by Morgan James Publishing. Morgan James and The Entrepreneurial Publisher are trademarks of Morgan James, LLC. www.MorganJamesPublishing.com

The Morgan James Speakers Group can bring authors to your live event. For more information or to book an event visit The Morgan James Speakers Group at www.TheMorganJamesSpeakersGroup.com.

Shelfie

A **free** eBook edition is available with the purchase of this print book.

CLEARLY PRINT YOUR NAME ABOVE IN UPPER CASE

Instructions to claim your free eBook edition:
1. Download the Shelfie app for Android or iOS
2. Write your name in **UPPER CASE** above
3. Use the Shelfie app to submit a photo
4. Download your eBook to any device

ISBN 978-1-68350-031-5 paperback
ISBN 978-1-68350-032-2 eBook
ISBN 978-1-68350-033-9 bundle
Library of Congress Control Number:
2016905648

Cover Design by:
Rachel Lopez
www.r2cdesign.com

Interior Design by:
Bonnie Bushman
The Whole Caboodle Graphic Design

In an effort to support local communities and raise awareness and funds, Morgan James Publishing donates a percentage of all book sales for the life of each book to Habitat for Humanity Peninsula and Greater Williamsburg.

Get involved today, visit
www.MorganJamesBuilds.com

Habitat
for Humanity®
Peninsula and
Greater Williamsburg
Building Partner

TABLE OF CONTENTS

INTRODUCTION
YOSSELIN'S BROKENNESS

We met Yosselin in January. Yosselin was the reason I thought we needed the word *bigger*. She sat next to my daughter, Ella, in their first grade classroom, which is a miracle itself because I never intended to put Ella in school. I spent the entire summer wrestling with God over the school issue. I assumed my surrender was coming in the form of doing whatever it took to educate my children outside of the public school system, but the lack of peace inside left me wondering what God was trying to say.

I didn't want to ask Him what He wanted from me because I didn't want to know. I was scared. Having had a not so great experience growing up in public schools I feared the same for my children. I wanted to protect them. Turns out, the best protection I could give them was my obedience to the plans of the Father.

My surrender came in the shape of Wyandot Early Childhood School, where Ella would soon start first grade. Ella and Yosselin became quick friends. The two sat next to each other in class. They shared pencils, books, stories and a future, *bigger* than they could ever have dreamed.

In November, Yosselin started missing school. It didn't take long for Ella to notice the absence of her friend. Every day, Ella came home from school, "Mom, Yosselin wasn't in school today. Mom, Yosselin was sick again. Mom, do you think she is on vacation? Mom, do you think she is okay? Mom, will you call Ms. O'Keefe and see if Yosselin is alright?" On and on she went, every day, relentlessly. Something wasn't right and Ella sensed it.

I sensed it too, which was part of the reason I didn't want to ask. Knowledge brought responsibility and responsibility scared me. As long as I remained oblivious to what was going on, I didn't have to get involved. Eventually Ella's persistence wore me down and I e-mailed Marilyn, the girls' teacher, "Hi, Marilyn, Ella has come home every day for a few weeks now concerned about Yosselin and her absence. I know you might not be able to talk about what's going on, but we would love to know if there is anything we could do to help this family."

Rounding the corner of the girl's school, I noticed Marilyn nervously waiting for me by the lockers. I could tell by the look on her face things were not okay. My heart sank deep into my stomach. Every part of me wanted to turn around and not hear whatever it was she was about to tell me. She pulled me aside and let me in on what was going on with Yosselin. Ella's classmate had cancer. Osteosarcoma. The rapidly growing bone cancer was taking up seven inches of her femur and she had numerous nodes in each lung. The cancer had spread so quickly doctors immediately pulled her out of school and started her on chemo. Her future was unknown at this point. They were in for the fight of their lives.

Reading through chapter one of Nehemiah in preparation for an upcoming talk, God gave me a glimpse inside the process Nehemiah walked from brokenness to *bigger*. Brokenness always lead to *bigger* when placed in the hands of the Master Rebuilder. God never intends to leave us sitting in what's broken. He has so much in store for us, but we cannot expect to simply wake up one day at the *bigger* place. *Bigger* comes when we surrender to His rebuilding process. The process involves following plans we don't have the privilege of holding. He has them. He has always had them and our Master Rebuilder invites us to journey with Him through His process of rebuilding.

Partnering with Yosselin and her family was demanding, both emotionally and mentally, but we knew what we had been promised. There is nothing to big. Our God is more than capable. He is ready and able and willing to rescue His children. We didn't know where we were going. We simply had a dream in our heart and a word from the Lord. *"If you will trust me to do this, I will rebuild to be more than you could ever ask or imagine possible."*

That's the thing about *Bigger*. It represents land we have yet to conquer. It demands faith and trust, hope and belief. It brings on a new understanding of God and the power He holds. It offers deeper intimacy and a supernatural ability to trust what we do not know in the hands of the Almighty. *Bigger* is abundance. It's more of Him, more freedom, more identity, more authority, and more power. It is best represented in being at the end of ourselves, our resources, our minds and most importantly, the end of our will. At these places of intense brokenness we have only just begun to see and experience who He really is.

Whether he knew it or not, Nehemiah walked the process. He journeyed from brokenness to *bigger*. He cried hard, prayed hard, worked hard, and in the end he experienced more of God than he ever thought possible, externally and internally.

This Bible study is an invitation for you to walk from brokenness to *bigger*. No matter how deep or how shallow the place we start, God always has more in store for us. Too many times we place a Band-Aid over what's broken as a way to avoid pain. The problem is, we were never meant to live with Band-Aids. We were meant to live in wholeness and healing. Because of Band-Aids we have become a culture of settlers. We settle down in the small and accept what we know, when with a little work, *bigger* is right on the other side. There is nothing beyond His grace. Nothing's too far gone for His redemption. We surrender to Jesus and then He invites us into a process of transformation, a process of becoming more and more like Him. Not because we need to be Him, but because we need to reflect Him.

It's not necessarily about the word *bigger* as much as it is the concept. *Bigger* is the word the Father spoke over me when I called out for His help. Sitting before the broken, at the end of myself, I needed something. I needed God. I needed Him to be *bigger*, to move *bigger*, to grow me *bigger*. I needed Him to rebuild the ruins I faced. The concept works for anyone willing to surrender the broken to the Master Rebuilder. Surrender to the idea that God has more for you (both inwardly and outwardly) than where you are. He doesn't intend to leave you sitting. Use whatever word you need, but find Him there, in the broken, and learn how to believe in your rebuilding.

Bigger isn't definable because it's personal. It's between you and Him. What He has for you is different than what He has for me. I rarely hand Him something broken and know the place He will lead me as we rebuild. Nor do I know the length of time we will work together on the project. All I know is, He is near and I can trust Him. I don't know what God wants to do with the brokenness in your life right now, but Ephesians 3:20, tells me He wants to do something and it's more than you can imagine. I don't know what you might look like on the other side of transformation, but I know you will be different. Yosselin got a new house and through it I received a *bigger* understanding of how much God loves us and the power of His furious love. Each time around we glean something new, something different, something life changing.

You should note this: sometimes the places the Lord leads on this rebuilding journey aren't always luxurious. I've followed him to some pretty rocky places. Places I never asked to go and never imagined myself in. I followed in faith that He was working, redeeming, rebuilding. I followed because I believe in the process. I believe brokenness, in the hands of Jesus, always leads to *bigger.* Don't bail because it looks hard. Don't quit because it doesn't make sense to your finite human mind. Follow Him there because *bigger* is there. He will not lead you somewhere to leave you somewhere. It is for a reason, for a purpose and you will be better off having gone.

Nehemiah was called to quit his high caliber job, working for the King, and secretly go into Jerusalem for what appeared to be an impossible task. Throughout Scripture we often see the *bigger* invitation consisting of an intense, refining process. Regardless of what it looks like the promise is true, "He is able to do immeasurably more than all we ask or imagine, according to his power that is at work within us." (Eph. 3:20)

He has more for you too. Don't settle for life in spite of the broken pieces. Surrender to transformation. Call out to Him, sit with Him, learn to trust Him, follow Him out of brokenness and into the rewarding process of rebuilding. Believe in Jesus. Believe in *bigger*. Those Band-Aids hiding your brokenness are ineffective. He never intended for you to keep them on this long. They will not do for you what He will do for you. What if over the course of these eight weeks we take a few of them off, together? Will you let the wall fall down? Will you trust His plans to rebuild? He's calling you to *bigger*. Can you hear Him?

Below are a few instructions/suggestions for your time in this workbook. Read over them carefully to ensure your journey is as rich as possible.

Days 1-4 will deal directly with what's broken in your life, while day 5 will offer you the opportunity to step out and help someone else on their broken journey.

It's truth; we travel better together. Before each personal section is a small group section. The journey from broken to *bigger* is hard enough, don't make the mistake of going it alone. We need each other and will talk more about that during week six, but for now, please consider teaming up with friends, relatives, a spouse or even complete strangers to spur one another on. The group questions are meant to be conversation starters. Use some of them, use all of them, only use one of them, but talk. Share your journey. Share your hurts, your disappointments and your fears. Become a fan of saying things out loud. It's amazing the power our thoughts hold over us. Wrestle through hard emotions, intense questions and unknown answers. We serve a God big enough to handle our honest struggle to understand. He isn't thrown off by our questions. In fact, often times during those questions, He shows up *bigger* than ever. Finally, when working in a group, don't be an answer-giver, be a question-asker. The truth is we don't know how God wants to rebuild the people around us. Only He has the plan. Only He knows the way. Our job is to work together to hear and follow Him. This means, when walking next to someone your job is not to direct in rebuilding, but to guide toward Jesus. Sometimes it is hard to hear in the midst of our own pain. Listen with them, sit beside them and cry for them. Jesus will be nearby. It's part of His promise. In our brokenness we need Him. He is the answer we seek. Use this study to become a person who is most comfortable letting Jesus be the answer.

Let's get started!

OUR BROKEN LIVES
Book Chapters: 1-3

├────────────────────┤

Small Group Discussion Guide

When you think of the word broken what is the first thing that comes to your mind?

_____

_____

_____

_____

What, if anything, in your life feels broken right now?

_____

_____

_____

_____

Read Isaiah 57:15 together. Where does God say He lives?

_____

_____

_____

_____

I want to be where the broken are because that's exactly where Jesus lives. If God moved into your city, where do you imagine Him spending most of His time? Why?

_____

_____

_____

_____

Read Ephesians 3:14-20. This is Paul's prayer for the Church of Ephesus. What part of this prayer grabs your attention the most?

_____

_____

_____

_____

Paul wants his friends, in Ephesus, to know God has so much more for them. He wants them to believe in the bigger. Is there an area in your life where you struggle to believe God has more in store for you?

Week 1—Personal Study Guide

Sometimes it's hard to see things for what they really are. There are days it takes everything I have to keep my head above water and other days when the worst struggle I face concerns who used the last bit of my favorite creamer or who forgot to put the lid back on the toothpaste!

On the hard days, struggling not to go under, I find myself clinging to God and His promises of *bigger* like never before. Other times I am less focused on my struggle and more available to notice the brokenness in the lives of others, like we did when we partnered with Yosselin, her cancer, and her desperate need for a new living space. There are always opportunities in brokenness to be available for others. Recognizing we are broken people, living in a broken world, frees us up to be honest and helpful with one another. Everyone has a story and everyone with a story battles to press forward.

When the personal battles we fight threaten to capsize us, they might require our fullest attention. During these times it is okay to use our best energy to find Jesus and connect with Him to better keep our head above water. Trying to help people experience what we are not experiencing ourselves can be exhausting. It's a both/and—we have a responsibility to reach out and help others, but we also have a responsibility to be aware of where we are personally. Believe it or not, we sometimes miss out on experiencing *bigger* by only focusing on the brokenness of others and never taking time to listen to what God might be saying to us. There's also something powerful that happens when we allow our brokenness to shine through and we begin to see God partnering with us in spite of it. Our brokenness does not disqualify us. It is actually our what qualifies us. Brokenness in us demands the help of the Spirit of God through us. When His power shines into our weakness, His light shines through our cracks and people see His glory.

God is multifaceted. He can do a work in us and through us, all at the same time. It is in the rhythm of spending intimate time with Him building relationship, time in community with others, and time out in the world we best experience *bigger,* both in and around us. A relationship exists where we fully live recognizing and responding to the voice of God on behalf of our own brokenness, while at the same time recognizing and responding to Him concerning the brokenness of others. Our broken state of being does not push Him away. In fact, it is often from this place we find him most and serve Him best.

God is not interested in what we can do for Him. He is interested in what we can do with Him. It is always about relationship. It's a partnership. Working together, Him and us, we grow, deeper and wider. Needing Him is what qualifies us. You are not qualified because of anything you've done. Likewise, you are not disqualified because of anything you've done. You are qualified because of Him. He qualifies you. And He loves His job. He loves to qualify you. He loves being together, building together and journeying forward.

Now, it's your turn, these pages are totally for you. Our response to God during broken times will determine how our journey through the desert will result in *bigger* spiritual growth or spiritual decline. It helps me to write. Words often bring healing. Try it. Write your brokenness openly all over these pages. Please don't hold back. If you have to find a secret place to hide this book for now, then do it. I'm believing on the other side of this journey healing will feel so rich, you won't hesitate to let people read these pages because they will see Jesus all over them. God is biggest when we are most broken and His glory is shown all throughout our rebuilding process. So let's deal with the pain, wrestle with the words of His Word and step out into seemingly impossible situations. Let's push forward together and believe in what we won't always be able to see. Let's believe in *bigger*. Regardless of your situation, he has more for you. Let go of your disappointment, doubt, fear, restlessness and embrace His Spirit. Invite Him to do a deeper work in you from this moment on.

**And let us consider how we may spur one another
on toward love and good deeds. Hebrews 10:24**

In the box on the next page are a few important definitions. These are words we will use often together and it will help to be on the same page as we start our journey.

Broken—past participle of break- having been fractured or damaged and no longer in one piece or in working order.

Brokenness—After something has been broken, but before it has been put back together.

Restoration—the act of restoring; renewal, revival, or reestablishment.

Walls—any of various permanent upright constructions having a length much greater than the thickness and presenting a continuous surface except where pierced by doors, windows, etc.: used for shelter, protection, or privacy. In our case walls represent something we have constructed for protection.

Redemption—an act of redeeming or atoning for a fault or mistake, or the state of being redeemed. deliverance; rescue.

Bigger—More than we've ever asked or imagined. Not necessarily physically (although sometimes it may be) but spiritually. Ephesians 3:14-20. Bigger is defined based upon the situation and circumstances and always dependent upon the plans of the Father.

Keep these definitions close to you. Come back to them often. They will help as you partner with the Father and begin your rebuilding process.

"For this reason I kneel before the Father, from whom every family in heaven and on earth derives its name. I pray that out of his glorious riches he may strengthen you with power through his Spirit in your inner being, so that Christ may dwell in your hearts through faith. And I pray that you, being rooted and established in love, may have power, together with all the Lord's holy people, to grasp how wide and long and high and deep is the love of Christ, and to know this love that surpasses knowledge—that you may be filled to the measure of all the fullness of God. Now to him who is able to do immeasurably more than all we ask or imagine, according to his power that is at work within us, to him be glory in the church and in Christ Jesus throughout all generations, for ever and ever! Amen."
Ephesians 3:14-21

Day 1—Asking Hard Questions

I hesitated when we first found out what was going on with Yosselin. I wanted Yosselin to get to *bigger*, I wanted her to find healing, to experience the fullness of life without cancer and the benefits of a house not ransacked by flood damage, but I didn't want my family to get hurt on the way there. My girls had never experienced sickness; they hadn't known anyone with cancer, they were young and oblivious to a world full of brokenness. Yosselin's diagnosis was complicated and her recovery process very difficult. We're not talking about the flu here. She had stage-four osteosarcoma. There was a very real possibility she would not make it through this battle and for that I felt the need to build walls of protection around them.

Fearing future pain for my girls almost kept me from surrendering to *bigger*. Choosing to partner with God meant letting go of what I couldn't control. My maternal instinct longed for self-preservation and protection. My initial reaction was to stay where it was safe and avoid uncomfortable complications that come when we get involved with the brokenness happening around us. There was no way to walk with this family through the pain and not be affected. Their brokenness was going to move us, it was going to challenge us, it was going to force us outside of our comfort zone and in the end, one way or another, we would be different.

Brokenness in our own hands is a scary thing. But, brokenness in the hands of God is exactly the right thing. Brokenness always leads to *bigger* when placed in the hands of the Master Rebuilder. Following Him through the broken directly aligns us with His *bigger* promises. Removing Band-Aids and allowing walls to crumble quickly brings us to the end of ourselves and directly lines us up with the beginning of Him. There are only so many walls we can build before our resources run out, our talents cease and our strength drains. He has an unlimited number of resources available to those who will be broken before Him.

Sometimes brokenness comes out of nowhere. One-minute things are great and the next—everything has changed. Other times it is something we are subtly or even subconsciously unaware of. And then there are those days we attempt to convince ourselves we aren't the ones broken and we are just fine to spend the rest of our lives the way we are.

However it comes, when brokenness comes, it's hard.
Read Nehemiah chapter 1

What are the significant events unfolding in chapter 1? Who are the main characters?

_____

_____

_____

_____

The news of the broken down walls in Jerusalem and the poor state of God's people took Nehemiah's breath away. His pain for them overwhelmed him, forcing him to the ground. Nehemiah wept openly before the Lord. He didn't try to hide his heartache. He simply allowed it to break.

Have you ever been in a position like Nehemiah, where something just didn't feel right and you sensed brokenness? When his brother approached he knew something was wrong. Is there anywhere in your life you sense the need for some form of healing? Even if you don't know what it is quite yet, that's okay. What is your normal response to these type of feelings?

_____

_____

_____

_____

_____

Nehemiah wasn't afraid to ask the hard question. If his gut instinct was right, then he knew heartbreak was possible. But the fear of the unknown didn't keep him from opening his mouth. He asked anyway. The truth is we don't have to settle for brokenness. Through Jesus our lives have been redeemed and are continually being built to reflect more and more of His glory. If we will surrender to His process of rebuilding then nothing is for nothing and everything is possible.

Where in your life have you settled into the lie of "this is just the way it is?"

Spend a few minutes in prayer and ask God about this lie. Write down anything you feel Him speaking to you.

_____

_____

_____

_____

Some of my most significant spiritual growth has come after asking God hard questions. Not hard as in long, lengthy, too complicated to understand questions, but hard as in, "I'm not sure I want to hear the answer to these questions." If I'm honest with you there are times when I don't ask God what He thinks about my marriage, my children or my friendships because I don't want to face the reality of what He might say.

Have you ever avoided a topic to simply avoid hearing what God thinks? What was it you were afraid to ask? What were you trying to avoid hearing?

_____

_____

_____

_____

In Psalm 139:23-24, David asks God a hard question. What is it?

_____

_____

_____

_____

Maybe you already know what's broken in your life, maybe you don't. Either way, take a few minutes and ask God to show you what He sees. Record any of your insights below.

_____

_____

_____

_____

Day 2—Broken-Hearted

It's probably safe to say Nehemiah never saw it coming. He wasn't even with God's people when they were freed from captivity and allowed to go back to their broken-down city. Nehemiah was busy being the cupbearer to the King of Persia. He was living his life, minding his own business when God showed up, out of nowhere, and broke his heart into a million pieces.

Once released from captivity, the Israelites returned to their city, only to realize the walls, offering protection from their surrounding enemies, had been torn down. With no walls, they would easily fall victim to whomever decided to take advantage of them. With a lack of resources and leadership, there seemed to be no opportunity to rebuild and restore order to this once-vibrant community. Perhaps they were better off as slaves. At least when they were enslaved they had food and protection.

Have you ever thought to yourself, "I was better off *insert place you used to be here.*" Where was that place you thought you were better off?

_____

_____

_____

_____

_____

_____

_____

What makes you think you might have been better off in this place?

_____

_____

_____

_____

_____

_____

_____

Is this place a broken place?

_____

_____

_____

_____

Only one day into your study do you think God ever intends to leave someone in their broken place?

_____

_____

_____

_____

Nehemiah was not better off distanced from the reality of what was going on back home. He was not better off as the cupbearer to the King. He was better off in the broken, because God lives and moves and works in the broken. Brokenness always leads to *bigger* when placed in the hands of the Ultimate Rebuilder. God wants to rebuild what has been broken in your life, but first you must admit the best place for you is amongst the broken pieces. What are the broken pieces in your life right now?

_____

_____

_____

_____

Are you the type of person who shares these pieces with others or do you keep them to yourself? When is the last time you told someone you were broken?

_____

_____

_____

_____

Do you trust God will meet you in what's broken?

"I live in the high and holy places, but also with the low-spirited, the spirit-crushed, and what I do is put new spirit in them, get them up and on their feet again."

Isaiah 57:15

Day 3—Brokenness in the Bible

Brokenness is everywhere. It is the story all throughout the Bible; broken people encountering Jesus and finding redemption. You can't truly encounter Jesus and stay the same. Sitting in our brokenness gives Him time to show up. When He shows up everything changes. With Him building on our behalf, healing is imminent.

Read the story of Jairus in Luke 8:40-56.

Jairus was a synagogue ruler. This meant, even though he had probably witnessed some of Jesus' miracles, he would still have had a hard time calling Jesus, the Messiah. Until, that is, the day brokenness hit too close to home and everything changed for this ruler. Jairus' twelve-year-old daughter was dying and he was desperate. Being a synagogue ruler, he spent a large part of his day fixing things, but he could not fix this. He could not heal the sick. He didn't know how to overcome death. And so as his world came crashing down around him, he ran to Jesus. In his desperation, he cried out for Jesus to fix the broken before him.

At the end of himself, Jairus found Jesus. What did Jairus do when he found Jesus?

_____

_____

_____

_____

What was Jesus' response to Jairus?

_____

_____

_____

_____

Does Jesus' response bring you hope? Why?

_____

_____

_____

When was the last time you felt as though you were at the end of yourself?

_____

_____

_____

_____

At the end of yourself did you run to Jesus? Did you find Him? What was His response to you? What was your response to Him?

_____

_____

_____

_____

Coming to the end of ourselves is exactly where we need to be. At the end of ourselves we are only at the very beginning of Him. Jesus does His best work when we throw up our hands in defeat. He is the God of impossibilities and He wants us to depend on Him fully. It's okay to be scared. It's okay to not fully understand. It's okay to hurt, but don't allow those feelings to keep you from the one person who sees past what you see. Bring your stuff to Jesus and give Him time to step into what's broken.

Day 4—I'm broken

The easy thing about brokenness is it is everywhere. We live in a broken world, with broken people. Marriages are broken. Children are broken. Friendships are broken. Jobs are broken. Diseases are broken. With brokenness surrounding us at all times, there will always be opportunity to surrender to God's process of rebuilding for bigger.

Jesus wants to meet you in your brokenness. It doesn't matter what kind. It doesn't matter where or how or when it happened. The details aren't important. What you do with the heartbreak is what really matters. He never intended for you to walk it out alone. He has a plan. He has already prepared a way. To find Him, you must recognize what's broken, sit down and look up to accept His outstretched hand.

Unfortunately we live in a world of Band-Aids. Instead of letting the walls fall and the broken be broken, we have grown accustomed to doing whatever it takes to hold them together. We bandage up our wounds out of fear, rejection, pain or isolation. We grab for the biggest, most efficient bandages and wrap up all levels of brokenness in an effort to avoid the consequences of a collapsed wall.

Let's spend our time together today removing the Band-Aids from the broken walls in our lives. A Band-Aid is a material holding two or more broken pieces together. The Band-Aid doesn't bring healing; there is nothing special within it. It simply adheres to the broken and allows it to appear different than before. Eventually the Band-Aid has to come off so true healing can begin.

Are there areas of your life where you have placed Band-Aids in hopes of keeping things together? If so, name a few below.

_____

_____

_____

_____

What kind of aid are those Band-Aids providing for your life right now?

_____

_____

God doesn't do Band-Aids. He doesn't do partial. He's not a fan of temporary. Band-Aids can only do so much. They aren't the real deal, they are a cover up and hiding what's broken blocks the very wound in need of healing. Band-Aids might work for a while, but eventually they wear down. Eventually they fall off. Eventually they stop sticking. Eventually they become the very thing keeping the cut from receiving the healing it needs.

God promises to rebuild what's been broken in our lives. Write Proverbs 3:5-6 below.

_____

_____

_____

Do you really believe God can take what's broken in your life and make it *bigger*? If so, what is your hope for your brokenness?

_____

_____

_____

Write Ephesians 3:20 below.

_____

_____

_____

This passage says God can do exceedingly and abundantly more than we ever imagined possible with our lives, our circumstances, our relationships and even our futures. If this is true, then it is the promise of *bigger*. If the very broken thing in your life were to be restored to *bigger,* what might it look like?

_____

_____

_____

Day 5—Challenge Day—Brokenness in the World

Brokenness is everywhere. It's in my house, in my family, in my friends. I can hop in my car, drive a few miles into the city and see it on every street. Hamilton is one of the most dangerous places to live in Ohio. Your chance of becoming a victim of crime in Hamilton is one in twelve. With so much brokenness, the temptation to look past it is real. What can I really do anyway? It's too much. Too far gone. I don't have enough resources. What I could do wouldn't even equal a drop in the bucket.

We might live in a broken world, but we do not serve a broken God. If we believe in *bigger* and we believe brokenness always leads to *bigger* when placed in the hands of the Master Rebuilder, then our job is to come alongside the brokenness in others and open their eyes to the *bigger* promises of God.

Reread Nehemiah 1 again and answer the following questions.

Where was Nehemiah when he heard about the news of his people?

_____

_____

_____

_____

_____

How did He find out about the broken down walls?

_____

_____

_____

_____

What was his response to the news?

_____

_____

_____

_____

When is the last time you allowed someone else's brokenness put you on the ground?

_____

_____

_____

_____

Think about your day, where you live, with whom you interact, where you work. Is there a specific place where brokenness calls out to you? A place where you could go and do your part to aid in the rebuilding process of others? We don't have to have it all together to be a conduit for Jesus' rebuilding. We simply have to be willing to step out. It is often in stepping out we also find the healing we are working toward.

What is one step you can take over the next few days to join someone in his or her brokenness and point him or her toward *bigger*?

_____

_____

_____

_____

_____

AT THE END

Book Chapters: 4-6

├────────────────────────────┤

Small Group Discussion Guide

We sometimes use Band-Aids to keep our broken walls standing. The problem is Band-Aids don't last. Eventually they wear down and fall off. What have you put a Band-Aid on before only to find it failing to hold the pieces together fully?

_____

_____

_____

Without Band-Aids the broken walls representing our lives fall down. What about falling walls scares you the most?

_____

_____

_____

Where in your community have you accepted Band-Aids instead of choosing to step in and be involved in the brokenness of others?

_____

_____

_____

What's one thing you could do to shine some light into these broken places?

_____

_____

_____

_____

Why do we hide in the dark when we know healing only happens in the light?

_____

_____

_____

_____

Read John 8:12. What does Jesus refer to himself as?

_____

_____

_____

_____

Read Ephesians 5:14. According to this passage what happens in the light?

_____

_____

_____

_____

Before Jesus we are in the dark. The light shines into the darkness and the darkness has two choices; go deeper into the dark so as to avoid exposure or come fully into the light and be exposed. Discuss the difference between the two? Have you ever been guilty of running deeper in avoidance? If so, what happened? What finally made you come fully into the light?

_____

_____

_____

Week 2—Personal Study Guide

Bigger has the best beginnings in places of helplessness. Coming to the end of ourselves leaves us perfectly positioned for the *bigger* things of God. Brokenness does a good job of ending us. It swiftly forces even the most confident person into an open posture. When the walls come down around us, truth is always exposed. In this posture we are right where He needs us to be.

Fear of the truth is often the very thing preventing us from experiencing the *bigger* we were created for. I fear the unknown. I fear the disapproval of those around me and with that comes a colossal fear of failure. I have spent much of my life piecing brokenness back together in the dark, slapping on Band-Aids and praying they hold up through the rain. The biggest problem – God doesn't fix what we won't admit is broken.

Truth leads to transformation.

You can do this. You can come to the end of yourself and be okay. It's not going to be easy. It might get ugly, but don't let any of that stop you. It's a game you're guaranteed to win. All you have to do is step on the field. Our victory comes through actively engaging His promises. So stop trying to figure out how this ends. You win because He won. Get all the way in. It will be the best mess you've ever let go of.

Day 1—Letting it Go Deep

Nehemiah might have wished he could take it back, but it was too late: the look on Hanani's face said it all. It's never easy to let someone in on news you know is going to hurt, but Hanani didn't hide what was going on to protect Nehemiah. He knew if there were any hope for healing and restoration he had to lay it all on the table. The truth was, things were not good, the walls were broken and the future of God's people uncertain. Without a miracle, the Israelites were doomed to destruction.

Write Nehemiah 1:4.

_____

_____

_____

_____

Nehemiah's people were in distress and Nehemiah felt their fear. He sensed their insecurities and understood their shame. He took their brokenness personally, much like God does for us. God takes our pain seriously. He knows it. He feels it. His Son lived it. Our pain is His pain because He carries it for us. It's amazing what happens when we take other people's brokenness personally, when we feel their pain, understand their hurts and weep over the destruction.

Write Isaiah 53:4 below.

_____

_____

_____

_____

We serve a God of *bigger*. He is not intimidated with the broken pieces in our lives. They don't look so overwhelmingly intense to Him. Instead of sharp, painful shards of glass He sees the perfect rebuilding materials. You can trust Him with what's broken. Last week we recognized our brokenness. We recognized how God won't heal what we don't admit is broken. If we want to accept His promise of more, if we want a life of *bigger,* then we must be willing to sit in the broken and call out to Him.

What was the brokenness you admitted to last week?

_____

_____

_____

_____

Did you sense a promise of *bigger* to be claimed over this brokenness? What might it look like if God took these broken pieces and did more than you could ever ask or imagine with them?

_____

_____

_____

_____

Jesus is less concerned with what's been broken and more concerned with the heart of the person in front of Him. Read the story below and answer the following questions. Remember it has little to do with the level of brokenness and everything to do with loving the broken person.

Read Luke 7:36-50.

Where was Jesus in this story?

_____

_____

_____

_____

Who showed up uninvited to their dinner?

_____

_____

_____

_____

Describe this woman's reaction to Jesus below.

_____

_____

_____

_____

The woman could not contain herself in the presence of Jesus. He did something for her no one had ever done before. Through Him, she found freedom. She found mercy and redemption. Through Him, her brokenness felt different. In His presence, she let loose. Breaking her alabaster jar (probably one of the most expensive items she owned) she soaked his feet with her tears and wiped them clean with her hair. Was it possible that as she came to the end of herself, she was beginning to find hope for a new future? Was *bigger* on the horizon? Jesus scolded the Pharisees for the way they treated Him, but what did he say about the woman?

_____

_____

_____

_____

If you were this woman, how would it feel to stand in front of Jesus right now? What are some of the things you might do? What might you say?

_____

_____

_____

_____

"And we know that in all things God works for the good of those who love him, who have been called according to his purpose."
Romans 8:28

Day 2—Sitting Down to Weep

Some people classify weeping as a sign of weakness, but in Nehemiah's case it was a sign of strength. Upon receiving the news of the broken, the Bible says he sat down and wept openly.

How do you view weeping?

_____

_____

_____

_____

When's the last time you sat down and had a good cry over something causing you pain?

_____

_____

_____

_____

Sitting down and weeping enables us to admit weakness. Bowing low is a sign of humility. By bowing to a king, you say that he is greater than you. Sitting now, it is easy to see my past pride pushing me to rebuild the walls in my life. My pride wanted to come off different than I was. My arrogance allowed me to blame others and resist the vulnerability of being exposed. It was easier to hide than to admit I was broken.

Write Psalm 25:9.

_____

_____

_____

_____

Pride doesn't work in the *bigger* because pride is all about us and *bigger* is all about God. When we allow our brokenness to show for what it is, it keeps us living in a state of humility. When light shines into what's broken it takes time for our eyes to adjust. Pride pushes us to turn the lights back off and keep the truth from being exposed. It lies and says we don't need adjustment. But, God doesn't put things back together in the dark.

It was a Jewish custom to sit down when mourning. *Shivah* is known as the "7 day period of mourning." When a Jewish family loses a loved one, they work really hard to plan and carry out all of the tasks for the funeral but once the funeral ends and the dead are buried they enter into the *Shivah*. The *Shivah* lasts up to 7 days. The participating Jews would suspend all normal daily activities and openly mourn over the loss they experienced. They even called it "Sitting Shivah." For days they wrestle through pain and mourn the memories. Only after the seven days were over would they return to normal activities.

We live in a culture that doesn't sit. Hard times hit and we do whatever it takes to stay standing. Standing up leave us in a position of action. Standing over our brokenness we look down and figure out how the pieces go back together in an orderly fashion.

But when we sit, we invite Him in. When we sit, He runs to us.

Write Psalm 147:3 below.

_____

_____

_____

Spend the remainder of your time sitting in your brokenness. Close your eyes and visualize yourself *"Sitting Shivah."* If I sat for seven days each time my heart was broken, I would save myself a lot of time. After seven days of sitting and mourning and crying out to God, I'm a different person and I have what I need to move forward. You might even need to rip off another Band-Aid. If so rip it. Let the wall fall and then have a seat.

After you have been silent and still before the Lord for a few minutes, reflect on some of the questions below.

What was the brokenness you sat down in?

_____

_____

_____

What did it feel like to sit?

_____

_____

_____

_____

Did you connect with Jesus as you sat? If so, what did He say?

_____

_____

_____

_____

If you were uncomfortable, what did you do?

_____

_____

_____

_____

Do you feel like this is something you could do in front of other people? (Would you be willing for them to see you sitting in something so broken?)

_____

_____

_____

_____

"Sitting Shivah" lasts for seven days. Seven full days of doing nothing so you could get to the deepest parts of the pain. Reflect on how sitting in what's broken before working through it can be beneficial?

_____

_____

_____

_____

Day 3—Look Up from the Pain

Something powerful happens as we sit down. Sitting makes surrender easier. As I sit in what's broken, I somehow find the strength to look up and look around. Looking around, I notice a few things.

First, I notice, I'm not the only one broken. There are cities of broken people, towns of broken pieces, lying all around me. Second, there is a shadow standing over me. I may be sitting, helpless and scared, but He is standing over me ready and willing to help.

It is in our brokenness we are most open to God, because it is there He has complete access. At no other time are the walls of our lives down, leaving us vulnerable to the Master's hands. In this place of vulnerability, we are able to rely on someone other than ourselves. God is in the business of rebuilding what's been broken, but He refuses to do it with Band-Aids. If we are patient, He will help us rebuild, one brick at a time, moving us from a place of brokenness to *bigger*.

I am no longer interested in the rebuilding process of Kristan. I am not the answer. I don't know the answer, but I know who does. Instead of rebuilding myself, I want to follow His lead. Together, one brick at a time, He will help me put the pieces exactly where they need to go according to His blueprints.

Write Psalm 34:18.

_____

_____

_____

_____

_____

Where is He for the brokenhearted?

_____

_____

_____

_____

_____

Write Psalm 73:26.

_____

_____

_____

_____

Who is He for the brokenhearted?

_____

_____

_____

_____

Write 2 Corinthians 12:9.

_____

_____

_____

_____

What does He promise the brokenhearted?

_____

_____

_____

Your God is near. He is standing right behind you. Notice His shadow. Notice how strong He is. As you're sitting, look up. The offer is for you. He will carry you. He will show you how to rebuild. He will even do the heavy lifting. He has *bigger* in store for you, if you are willing to surrender to the process of rebuilding. He promises to blow your mind.

Spend the remainder of your time talking to God about the rebuilding process. If you want to write your thoughts out, use the space below to do so.

_____

_____

_____

Day 4—Standing Up through the Pain

Fear of the truth is often the very thing keeping us from the *bigger*. Nehemiah wasn't afraid of the truth. The truth was, his people had gotten themselves into a mess. Freed from captivity, they were now in a city without walls. They were fully exposed to their surrounding enemies, leaving them open targets for whomever wanted to come in and take advantage of them. Perhaps they really would have been better off as slaves.

On my hardest days the same thought crosses my mind. Perhaps, I would have been better off to ignore the brokenness and continue on as if nothing mattered. If Nehemiah wished it then he only wished it for a second. The enemy works hard to convince us to stay in the dark, but we know our healing comes in the light.

Write John 12:35.

_____

_____

_____

_____

There is a path that leads to *bigger*, but in the dark we will not find it. *Bigger* is found in the light. Out in the open, where everyone can see, we are brought into our fullest healing and transformation.

Write John 1:5.

_____

_____

_____

_____

He is constantly shining His light into the dark corners of our lives. When the light shines into the dark, at first we may have to shield our eyes to not be overcome. The brightness of light can be somewhat terrifying. We must train ourselves to resist the urge to turn it back off.

What is hiding in the dark corners of your life right now?

_____

_____

_____

Do you see the light shining in on you?

_____

_____

_____

How does the brightness make you feel?

_____

_____

_____

Do you believe healing and wholeness will come by stepping into the light?

_____

_____

_____

We show what we believe by what we do. If you really believe your healing will come in the light, then step into it. Use the space below to write a prayer to God about coming out of the darkness. Don't skip over any part. Give Him the full mess. Every broken piece. Get up. Hand it to Him and start walking where He leads you.

_____

_____

_____

_____

_____

_____

_____

Day 5—Challenge Day—Helping Others Up

Sometimes we need a little help looking up. The weight of our brokenness rests heavy on our shoulders. Other people have helped me lift my head up when I couldn't do it on my own. They have come in, sat down next to me and worked to remind me of the *bigger* God promises over my life. Through their words and encouragement I've been able to look up.

Jesus helped his disciples keep their heads up. In Mark 6, we read the infamous story of the feeding of the 5,000. Jesus and His disciples had been out teaching all day and they were tired. Looking for a place to rest they tried to slip away unnoticed. Their plan backfired when the people realized Jesus was with them. Large crowds gathered, hungry to hear from the Rabbi. As dinnertime quickly approached the disciples panicked. With so many hungry people, chaos would surely break out. The disciples, thinking they were helping Jesus, suggested sending the people home so they could eat. They noticed the problem, but forgot the only answer needed was right in front of them.

Jesus is always the answer to the problems we face.

Luckily, Jesus hadn't forgotten. He knew he had the answer and He was going to remind His faithful followers.

Read Mark 6:37-44.

Jesus could have just stepped in and saved the day. He could have fixed the problem and moved on. But He knew better. He knew if He could open their eyes to the *bigger* and allow them to make their own way there (with His help, of course) what they would experience along the way would change them.

Is there someone in your life who could use a little support and encouragement for the *bigger* plans of God? Someone you could sit down next to and help lift up their eyes? A picture you could paint, a scripture you could recite or a letter you could write? What could you do this week to encourage someone else with finding their *bigger* in the middle of the broken?

_____

_____

PRAYER AND PARTNERSHIP
Book Chapters: 7-8

├─────────────────┤

Small Group Discussion Guide

Sometimes we choose to sit down and cry and other times life hits us so hard it takes our feet out from under us. Have you ever experienced the pain of unexpected loss?

_____

_____

_____

_____

How did you respond? How did you find Jesus and healing in your response?

_____

_____

_____

_____

Sitting down in general is hard. Sitting down and weeping in front of everyone can be excruciating. In today's busy world, making time to mourn loss is down right impossible. Do you feel like you have the space in your life to sit down for an extended period of time? What would happen if you did? If you don't have that space, how could you create space?

_____

_____

_____

_____

Read Romans 8:26-27. Have you ever been hurting so badly you didn't even have the words to pray? Since you couldn't pray, what did you do with your response?

_____

_____

_____

_____

How have others reached out to you during your greatest times of need? In what ways did their actions impact you for Jesus?

_____

_____

_____

_____

Have you experienced the Father reaching down and helping you stand in the midst of brokenness?

_____

_____

_____

_____

As a group come around those members who are hurting deeply right now. Offer up prayers on their behalf and help them sit.

Week 3—Personal Study Guide

This might be my favorite week. Prayer changes things. When our weeping moves to praying our brokenness moves to *bigger.* If we resist the urge to give up in brokenness and instead hand it over to God, He promises to use the pieces surrounding us as the building material for *bigger*—even when it feels impossible, even when it seems as though it's taking forever, even when the whole world looks to be against us. No matter what, if we will trust Jesus, brokenness always leads to *bigger.* God's ability doesn't run out simply because our ability to keep trying wanes. Weary moments are the moments we should find ourselves clinging to Him even more. Those are the moments we cannot lose sight of *bigger.* Our faith in His promises will empower us to keep moving.

When the initial pain of heartbreak hits, we react. If we let Him, God will take our reactions and turn them into responses. He doesn't plan to leave you where you are, but moving forward takes time. As the Master Rebuilder you can bet, He has a lot to tell you. Only He knows the way to where you are going. Jeremiah 33:3, "Call on me in prayer and I will answer you. I will show you great and mysterious things which you still do not know about." Call out to Him right where you are. He will answer you. He will find you. He sees you, hears you and intends to move you. Stay sitting long enough to hear Him. Sometimes that takes time so create extra space, space for just you and Him. In this journey, you will not be sorry, if the hardest work you do is the work you do to get yourself before Jesus in prayer and petition.

"Prayer is like love. Words pour at first. Then we are more silent and can communicate in monosyllables. In difficulties a gesture is enough, a word, or nothing at all- love is enough. Thus the time comes when words are superfluous...The soul converses with God with a single loving glance, although this may often be accompanied by dryness and suffering."1

---

1   Carlo Caretto, *Letters from the Desert* (Maryknoll, N.Y.: Orbis, 1972), p. 40.

Day 1—Fight or flight

Nehemiah didn't care who saw him. He didn't waste any time worrying about who was watching. He sat down, right in the middle of his brokenness and wept openly before God. Taking full advantage of his moment, he allowed the heartbreak to go deep. But then his cries turned to prayers and he desperately called out to God. The weight of his pain pushed him to the ground and the ground was exactly where he needed to be. From there he could more easily find his knees and his prayers could find the Father. Praying in the midst of heartbreak changes everything. It takes what we don't understand and aligns it with a God who fully understands.

Let's spend today breaking down the first part of Nehemiah's prayer.

Reread Nehemiah 1:5-11.

Praise His Awesomeness

Write Nehemiah 1:5a.

_____

_____

_____

_____

Yahweh was the name God gave Himself. It is a name above all names. *Yahweh* always was, and He always will be. He is absolute and constant. He is forever and His love will never end. *Yahweh* was Nehemiah's way of recognizing God's Sovereignty in his life. We do not serve a God bound to this earth. He is not limited in the ways we are limited. He is grand, He is mighty and in His might, He can do whatever He pleases. We can come to Him because He is *Yahweh,* our God of love. We count on Him because He is *Yahweh,* our God of heaven. No doubt Nehemiah struggled with the intensity of his pain. But his prayers served as a faithful reminder of the *bigger* God standing over him.

Write Isaiah 40:26.

_____

_____

_____

God does not lack in awesomeness; we lack in noticing His awesomeness.
When is the last time you stopped to simply notice the awesomeness of God?

_____

_____

_____

_____

What is the most awesome trait of the God you serve?

_____

_____

_____

_____

Even in the midst of tremendous pain, Nehemiah remembered how magnificent God was. It is easy to recognize the awesomeness of God in victory, but it is *necessary* to recognize it in heartbreak. Are you having a hard time recognizing God's awesomeness in the midst of your brokenness? Does His righteousness seem far from what you are weeping over? Pray it anyway. Cry, weep, wail, whatever it takes, just do it directed toward the Father. Our prayers to God in these moments will not return to us void. He will always be *bigger* than what you face.

Read the following verses and record the awesome things you learn about God.

Psalm 68:35

_____

_____

_____

Psalm 147:5

_____

_____

_____

Exodus 14:14

_____

_____

_____

Jeremiah 1:5

_____

_____

_____

Hebrews 4:13

_____

_____

_____

John 3:16

_____

_____

_____

_____

What is the most awesome thing God has done for you in your life?

_____

_____

_____

What is an awesome thing you would love for Him to do for you in your future?

_____

_____

_____

Take the space below and praise Him for His awesomeness.

_____

_____

_____

_____

Day 2—Confession

With the bar set and God in control, Nehemiah then transitioned his prayers toward repentance. He confessed his sins and the sins of his people. Nehemiah recognized Israel's sin and associated himself with his people. Not living there, no one would have blamed Nehemiah for not getting involved. But when the brokenness around us keeps God's people from experiencing *bigger*, we are called to get involved.

Other people's sin, what's broken in the lives of those surrounding us, is never larger than our own. It's simply different. Spending all of our time separating and blaming only leaves all of us missing out on the *bigger* God intends. Our fight is not against flesh and blood but against the powers of darkness. We are not each other's enemies. We are in this together. When something breaks, it hurts. Whether it's in my life or in yours. Whether I caused it or it happened to me. Let's not waste time getting tangled up in what doesn't matter.

Read Romans 3:10-12. What does this verse say about who is righteous?

_____

_____

_____

_____

Can we all agree no one is perfect? Can we admit we have all played a role in the brokenness surrounding us at some point in time? Nehemiah could have easily shaken his head and blamed the Israelites for the position they were in. They were the ones who turned against God. They were the ones who doubted. Nehemiah knew the truth: sin, regardless of whose it was and how it happened, only robbed everyone from *bigger*.

Now that we know no one is perfect, let's talk about what to do with our sin. Read 1 John 1:9.

What does He do when we confess our sin?

_____

_____

_____

Write Proverbs 28:13.

_____

_____

_____

_____

Hidden sin hides us. Hidden away we cannot openly confess. When real repentance happens inwardly, confession follows outwardly. A truly repentant heart isn't holding on to the pride of what others might think. We cannot move forward without confession. Hidden sin doesn't only hurt us it hurts everyone around us.

I'm a big fan of saying things out loud. There's something healthy about speaking it out. What we say out loud cannot have power over us any longer. God already knows anyways. He knows our sin. He knows our thoughts. He sees our actions. And even after all that, He waits for us still. When Addilyn (my 8 year old) gets in trouble the first thing I do is ask her to tell me what she did wrong. Saying it out loud makes it real.

Think about your life right now. Do you have unconfessed sin? Anything you are aware of but haven't been ready to speak out?

_____

_____

_____

_____

Read Proverbs 28:13 again (you just wrote it above). What does it say about unconfessed sin?

_____

_____

_____

_____

Take the space below and spend time in confession. Ask God to search your heart and show you anything offensive and then offer it up to Him for forgiveness.

Sometimes I like to take it one step further and call up a friend to confess to them as well. You don't have to do this for God's grace to work, but the more we talk about it the less power the enemy has to keep us hidden from *bigger*. Is it possible your healing has been delayed because you aren't willing to let someone off the hook for their sin? Forgiveness is tough. Sitting here typing right now I'm daily asking God to empower me to forgive the people who have greatly hurt our family this year. The loudest voice in unforgiveness is the enemy. He tangles my mind, my soul, my heart and my future up in His emotions instead of letting me walk forward into what God has for me. Your *bigger* might very well start when you let them go. Use the space below to confess any unforgivness you might have stored up in your heart.

_____

_____

_____

_____

Day 3—Promises, Promises

First, Nehemiah praised His awesomeness. Next, he confessed his sin and the sin of his people and finally he claimed God's promises. Moving away from the need to blame enables us to better see the *bigger* promises of God. When Nehemiah lifted his head what he saw in front of his eyes didn't line up with what he knew of God. Instead of hanging his head and assuming he must have misunderstood, he started reminding God of the promises He had made.

Read Nehemiah 1:8-9.

God's promises are true and He has them for you. Read the passages below and answer the questions.

Proverbs 3:5-6

What happens when you trust in the Lord with all your heart?

_____

_____

_____

_____

What would it look like for you to trust in the Lord with all your heart?

_____

_____

_____

_____

Matthew 11:28–29

What does this passage say about the load we carry with Christ?

_____

_____

_____

_____

This is something I try to remember always. If it's outwardly heavy, then it's not from Him. His yoke is easy and His burden is light. If His promises are active in your life, then you will not be burdened by a heavy load. The only heavy lifting He asks of us is internal lifting. It is the lifting of death to self. Once we have let go of ourselves and surrendered to a life of *bigger* the weight of obedience should prove lighter.

Do you have anything heavy in your life right now?

_____

_____

_____

_____

What would it look like for you to give your heavy load to Him?

_____

_____

_____

_____

Isaiah 40:29
What does He do for the weary?

_____

_____

_____

_____

Is it possible you need to ask Him to do this for you? If so, use the space below to do so.

_____

_____

_____

_____

I could keep going because there is a promise for everything. Proclaiming His promises is one of the most powerful ways we can pray. Confess your need to believe *bigger*. Focused on the promises of God, Nehemiah found the strength to begin conversations about moving forward. There is a time to sit and a time to move. As you sit before the Lord in prayer and fasting, know movement is coming. God is a God of movement. From the very beginning, He created us to be productive people. If you are calling out to Him, He will answer you. When He answers, be ready to respond. He never intends to leave us where we are and where He leads us is always better than where we've been.

He promises you so many things. Spend the rest of your time today claiming His promises for your life. Tell Him what you need. Tell Him what's heavy. Allow Him to lighten your load. Maybe there are promises from early on that you've pushed aside or decided to forget. Reclaim those today.

Nothing's for nothing when placed in the hands of the Master Rebuilder. God is the redeemer of all things broken.

Day 4—Prayer and Prophecies

"Prayers are prophecies. They are the best predictors of your spiritual future. Who you become is determined by how you pray. Ultimately, the transcript of your prayers becomes the script of your life."[2]

If this is true, then we should spend more time praying than we do working. Problem is, prayer is hard and to pretend it isn't, would be foolish. How would you pray differently if you really believe your prayers directly affect your future?

_____

_____

_____

_____

_____

I can't tell you how many times I've sat with people discouraged over not knowing how to pray. Matthew 18:3 says, "Truly I tell you, unless you change and become like little children, you will never enter the kingdom of heaven." Jesus loved children. It might have had something to do with their simplicity. Children simply say what they feel! How many times, have I jumped to cover one of my kid's mouths because I knew whatever was about to come out would be all levels of inappropriate! And how many nights do I sit by amazed at the simple, moving prayers of my children? We are the only measurers of our prayers. God is not counting how many times we say, "ummm." He's not keeping track of how we stutter our way through requests. We count, we judge, we wish to sound better, smarter, more convincing. What if we put all those insecurities aside and just shared from our heart? What if our prayers sounded less like a speech and more like a conversation?

Would you describe your prayer life as more of a conversation or a speech? What about prayer is your biggest struggle?

_____

_____

_____

---

2   Mark Batterson, *The Circle Maker* (Grand Rapids: Zondervan, 2011).

Read Revelation 3:20 and answer the following questions.
Where is Jesus standing?

_____

_____

_____

_____

What is He doing?

_____

_____

_____

_____

What does He promise to do?

_____

_____

_____

_____

A few years ago I started sitting at my kitchen table with Jesus. After my girls would go to school, I would move my Bible study, my journal and whatever materials I needed for the day and sit down with a big cup of coffee. Out loud I talked to Jesus and invited Him to sit at the table with me. Our conversations were awkward at first, as most are when we try getting to know someone on a new level. But I pushed through, thankful for His patience. There were days I didn't have anything to talk about. Instead of feeling like a failure and throwing in the towel I tried turning the tables on Him.

Write Jeremiah 33:3 below.

_____

_____

_____

_____

Jesus says He will answer us and when He does He will tell us things. We don't have to keep the conversation going. He promises to do His part if we pause long enough to let Him get a word in. He has so many things for us, so many things to tell us, to show us. Some of my favorite mornings are the mornings I sit down with a blank page in my journal and ask Him to tell me something I don't know. Why don't you practice it? Find a place where you can meet with Jesus. Let Him in the door, His hand might be tired from knocking. Sit down at the table with Him and give Him permission to speak into your life. Push past the scary silence, the best relationships always do, and see if He doesn't blow your mind with the depth of communication and understanding He has for you. Write down what He tells you. Take careful notes, even if you don't understand it. He has a way of bringing understanding back to us again.

Day 5—Challenge Day—Putting it on Paper

It's hard to believe in a muscle you can't see. Think about it, we go to the gym to shape our muscles. We want definition and strength. The first day in the weight room we strain and stress. With sweat dripping down our faces we push past the uncomfortable in order to obtain that which we know will come but cannot yet see. Those first few weeks in and out of the weight room your body aches, you struggle to walk up and down the stairs and even to sit on the toilet! All in the name of something you can't yet see, but trust pushes you to step nonetheless. The most powerful part of prayer is the day we start recognizing the fruit springing forth from it. Use the space below and write some of your struggles with prayer.

_____

_____

_____

_____

Now that you have a list, I want you to reread it. As you read, try to remember some of the things you've learned these past three weeks. As you remember, take your pen and put an X through your struggle.

Jesus loves to talk to you. The moments alone with my girls are few and far between. When I do get them I try to make the most of it and soak in every word. I want to keep them talking because when they talk we are connected. If I did all the talking then it would simply be me handing down the law to them, but if I create space and let them speak, through their words they start to let me in. I want in. I want into their longings, into their struggles, into their fears and into their joys. Even though, as their mom, I can force my way in, I desperately want their words to invite me in. Partnered together we are much more powerful.

God wants in. He wants to know you through your invitation. Whatever your prayer life has looked like in the past, today is a new day. "The faithful love of the Lord never ends! His mercies never cease. Great is his faithfulness; his mercies begin afresh each morning," (Lamentations 3:22-23 NLT).

What does it look like for you to go into the prayer room and start exercising those unseen muscles? Take a few minutes today to "schedule" time in the secret place with Jesus. If it's important to you, schedule it. What you do in the secret place with Jesus will affect your entire life. Write your "schedule" below.

_____

_____

_____

_____

_____

_____

_____

_____

_____

_____

_____

_____

_____

_____

_____

_____

_____

_____

Your Father, who sees what is done in secret, will reward you.
Matthew 6:4

TURNING AROUND
Book Chapter: 9

———————————————

Small Group Discussion Guide

How have you noticed yourself partnering with your prayers as you've journeyed toward *bigger?*

———————————————————————————
———————————————————————————
———————————————————————————
———————————————————————————

What is your biggest struggle in prayer?

———————————————————————————
———————————————————————————
———————————————————————————
———————————————————————————

Read Matthew 7:11. Are there things in life you haven't asked God for because you've feared He won't come through for you?

———————————————————————————
———————————————————————————
———————————————————————————

What does this passage say about how God intends to answer our prayers?

_____

_____

_____

_____

When I hesitate to ask God for something good it usually has a root of untruth wrapped around it. Luke 11:13 says, "If you then, though you are evil, know how to give good gifts to your children, how much more will your Father in heaven give the Holy Spirit to those who ask him!" I hope to give my girls good things in life. They might not always ask for what I intend to give, but when they do I will do whatever I can to make it happen. When I trust the heart of my Father and I believe He will withhold no good thing from me, then I can ask without fear and surrender my need to know the details. Do you ever feel like there is more behind your hesitation to ask God for things? Why might you be hesitating?

_____

_____

_____

_____

Are there specific prayers you are having a hard time praying right now? If so, what do you do? How do you pray when you don't know how to pray?

_____

_____

_____

_____

What does the word repentance mean to you?

_____

_____

_____

_____

Share a story of a time you repented, turned around and joined God for something. How did it turn out? What was the hardest part?

_____

_____

_____

_____

What role do other people play in your repentance?

_____

_____

_____

_____

Week 4—Personal Study Guide

In the past I always pictured repentance as some toiling, emotional event confirmed through excessive tears and drama. Repentance meant weeping, wailing, putting on sackcloth and ashes and burying your head in the pillow. And although all of these things represent a sorrowful, repentant heart and prove themselves to be necessary at times, repentance doesn't always have to be so dramatic. The simple definition of the word repent is to change one's mind. Concerning our faith and relationship with the Father, repentance is represented in two things.

Recognizing He is not facing the same direction we are and turning around to join Him. So many times we spend ourselves building where He is not. When we build without Him, we build in vain. What we put together is never guaranteed to last. In fact it is actually guaranteed not to last. Only He is forever and only His redemption never leaves us empty. It's likely He will lead you somewhere you didn't expect. Where He leads, follow. Turn away from what it is you want to focus on and turn yourself toward Him.

Be careful not to overstay your time in brokenness. We do this when we waste time facing the wrong direction. Wanting to move and moving are two different things. Repentance is belief in action. When we really believe God has more for us, then we don't hesitate to turn from where we are and join Him where He is.

Day 1—Turn and Repent
Start today off by reading Nehemiah 2:1-11.

How do we know Nehemiah repented?

_____

_____

_____

_____

Learning to look at repentance differently also teaches us to look at sin differently. If this journey is about partnership and partnership best happens when we join God in the rebuilding He is currently doing, then anything we do independently of Him keeps us from His good, pleasing and perfect will.

On our journey towards *bigger* we must pay careful attention to the direction we face. The Bible says, "God is always at work," (John 5:17). If He is the one with the master rebuilding plans, then we want to be building with Him and not off on our own somewhere.

Before God got Nehemiah's attention, where was he busy building?

_____

_____

_____

_____

I made a bad habit of rebuilding brokenness without God. With the best of intentions I worked hard on my walls and the walls of those surrounding me. I didn't like to see friends and family hurting. I hated watching them struggle through what felt like unnecessary pain and rejection. I wanted *bigger* for them, but I wanted it without the brokenness. Brokenness is the main ingredient for *bigger* and by covering it up, the false sense of security I offered paled in comparison to what the Father wanted. The journey from broken to *bigger* is a necessary part of the process and God is not in a hurry. He knows what He has reconstructed is worth all the time in the world and He is willing to give each piece the necessary space.

Reflecting back on your life, what are some of the things *you* have worked to rebuild instead of waiting for God?

_____

_____

_____

_____

What we build will never compare to what He builds. When He builds something, it stands because of the firm foundation from which is has been erected.

Write Matthew 7:24-27 in the space below. I know it's long, but writing something out takes our learning to a different level. Write it slowly, reading every word. When you are finished read it out loud, then answer the following questions.

_____

_____

_____

_____

_____

_____

_____

What grabbed your attention the most in this passage?

_____

_____

_____

_____

_____

Think about the house you live in. If I asked you to describe your house, you would most likely tell me about the location, the color, the design, the square footage, the size of the lot, and the number of bedrooms. Not many of us would jump right to the foundation, but the foundation is the most important part of our house. The foundation of Yosselin's house was ruined and ultimately what caused so much damage to the rest of the house. She needed a new house because of a broken foundation, not because of poor paint colors. Without a proper foundation, what we build will, in time, crumble. Proverbs 24:3 states, "By wisdom a house is built, and by understanding it is established." This is true not only of your house; it is also true of your life.

Verse 24 (NLT) says, "Anyone who listens to my teaching and follows it is wise, like a person who builds a house on solid rock." Read this verse and think about your healing process. What do Jesus' words mean for you on this journey?

He has the instructions and over time He will share them with us, but to obey we must first hear. How do you best hear from God?

Are there currently things standing in the way of your hearing?

How might you readjust your life to put yourself in a better place of listening?

God is working. He is building something *bigger* than you could ever imagine possible. You can trust Him to do something crazy good with your brokenness, but you have to turn around and join Him. Nehemiah saw God was moving elsewhere and he turned around. What does it look like for you to do that today?

_____

_____

_____

Day 2—Moments in Time

There are two different words for time in the Bible. *Chronos* refers to chronological or sequential time and *Kairos* refers to an exact moment in time. *Kairos* moments represent those little, unexpected interruptions. One moment we are headed one way and then out of nowhere something interrupts our path. What if we actually stopped, because those little interruptions might be from God? What if instead of doing our best to step over them and continue down our current path, we actually stopped and took notice? What if we asked God if it were Him trying to get our attention? What if we noticed Him doing something other than what we were doing and instead of pushing forward, we put ourselves aside, readjusted our lives and joined Him? Have you ever felt interrupted by God?

_____

_____

_____

_____

Joining Him in His interruptions will impact our future. Read Genesis 12:1-4. What was God's interruption (invitation) for Abraham?

_____

_____

_____

_____

How did he respond? What difference did it make?

_____

_____

_____

Read Matthew 4:19-22. What was God's interruption (invitation) for these disciples? How did they respond? What difference did it make?

_____

_____

_____

Think about your last few days. Spend some time reflecting on the events that took place. Were there any interruptions in your day? Any opportunities for you to join God and move in a different direction?

_____

_____

_____

_____

God interruptions can look like anything. They can be big or they can be small. They can affect only you or they can affect your entire family. Sometimes an interruption for me comes from the voice of an eight-year-old, little girl trying to get my attention while I'm typing away on the computer. In the past I would push through, ask for five more minutes to wrap up my work and then join her once I've finished. But what if I paused for a minute and ask if her interruption was an invitation to join God in something?

The other day I was out running. It was early in the morning but already scorching hot. I rounded the corner running towards my fourth mile marker. Out of the corner of my eye I noticed a lady sitting on her back porch. She was drinking her morning coffee and reading a magazine. As I ran by I felt a pull in my heart for this woman. I started praying for her, thinking maybe that would be enough, but I knew God was asking me to go and pray with her. If I'm honest, I really didn't want to. I was a sweaty mess and she was drinking her coffee. The last thing I want while I am drinking my coffee is some crazy, sweaty, jogger woman joining me, even if it is to talk about Jesus! I ran right by her ignoring the invitation on my heart. But about half a mile later I turned around. I didn't want to miss out on joining God in something. Making my way back to her house, I practiced my opening line. Ten minutes later, with tears in her eyes, she hugged me and said thank you for the tenth time and I was back on my way.

When your interruption came, what did you do with it?

_____

_____

_____

_____

What was the outcome?

_____

_____

_____

_____

Repentance for Nehemiah came in the form of an interruption. He was living his own life, separate from his people when his brother showed up with disturbing news. Nehemiah could have kept on going. No one would have blamed him. But, he didn't. He paused and allowed God to break his heart for his people back home. What Nehemiah did with this interruption changed everything.

_____

_____

_____

_____

What in this _bigger_ rebuilding process has been interrupting your life?

_____

_____

_____

_____

What do you feel the invitation might be?

_____

_____

_____

_____

Please be willing to keep going. God has so much in store for those of us who will allow Him to step in and change our course of direction. Trust Him, even when it doesn't make sense, even when people say it can't be done and the world seems to be against you. He has a way. He is the way. He will not fail you. You will not look back and wish you hadn't followed Him off course.

Day 3—What is God Really Saying?

Let's talk about how God is interrupting you through this study. What is the brokenness you are bringing before Him right now?

_____

_____

_____

_____

_____

Without Him how would you have responded to this pain? What are some of the things you might have done in the past? What might you have said to anyone close enough to see the broken? What feelings might you have felt while you worked to cover it in Band-Aids?

_____

_____

_____

_____

_____

With Him, how are you responding differently?

_____

_____

_____

_____

What is the biggest difference you have noticed when you respond with Him versus a time in the past when you responded without Him?

_____

_____

_____

_____

_____

There are days I hear God very clearly and then other days He seems silent. Look up the following passages and record what we learn about God's faithfulness to lead us out of our troubles by the sound of His voice.

Isaiah 30:21

_____

_____

_____

_____

John 10:27

_____

_____

_____

_____

Psalm 25:4-5

_____

_____

_____

_____

James 1:5

_____

_____

_____

_____

John 8:47

_____

_____

_____

_____

John 16:13

_____

_____

_____

_____

Which one of these passages encouraged you the most? What do you think God might be trying to say to you through His Word today?

_____

_____

_____

_____

Be encouraged friend, you serve a good God. Not only is He able to lead you through this process, He is eager to lead you through it. He will never leave you, never forsake you, never forget you and never betray you. He has good things for you. You can trust Him. He is a good guide, who is very capable of getting us to the _bigger_ He created us for.

Day 4—What Am I Going To Do?

If it were only about recognizing where God is working and what He might be saying, some of us would be in really good shape. I wish the same were true for recognizing we should exercise and eat healthfully. Unfortunately, what we think doesn't change us until it becomes what we do. I can recognize my need for exercise as long as I want, but until I actually lace up my shoes and head out for a run, I've not truly activated my belief. It's in our actual steps of movement, growth happens If we only ever had to find Him and never move ourselves to join Him we will never be stretched and without stretching there will be limited growth.

I learned something interesting the other day. The Hebrew word *Shema* is used to describe both hearing and obedience. It literally means to *hear and obey.* Some of the definitions are: understanding, taking heed, being obedient, and doing what is asked.

Think about it for a second. If I've asked Addilyn to do something, when do I know she's heard me? I know she's heard me when she obeys. Not after I've said it, not even after she's looked at me and sometimes even after she's responded. I really, only truly know she's heard me when she has taken the step to do what I've asked her to do.

Read the parable of the two sons in Matthew 21:28-32, what were the responses of each son?

_____

_____

_____

_____

What is the lesson Jesus shared with his listeners through this parable?

_____

_____

_____

_____

Share of a time you've heard something from God and not followed in action.

_____

_____

_____

_____

Doing implies hearing. Our actions show Him that we've heard what He's said. Knowing the greater meaning of the word *shemah* helps us understand why Jesus says, "He who has ears, let him hear,"(Mark 4:9). He is not simply calling us to sit on the couch and listen. He is calling us to stand up and take action with what we've heard. It also makes sense why revelation (hearing God) doesn't necessarily bring on more revelation. It's what we do with revelation (our response to what we've heard) that brings on more revelation. If we hear and respond He knows His instructions are not falling on deaf ears and He will say more.

Write James 1:22 below.

_____

_____

_____

_____

We've grown up in a culture focused on thinking, learning and the exercising of our own intellect. Jesus never meant for our own minds to get in the way and minimize the actual *doing* of his Word. If He has told you to do something, you can be sure He will wait for your response before He moves onto the next thing.

As a student ministry pastor for many years, I cannot tell you the amount of times I've sat down with teenagers and listened to them tell me how they don't know how to hear God. They would walk into my office defeated and discouraged over the lack of words between them and this Jesus, who supposedly wants to be their friend. My first question to them is always, "What's the last thing you remember God saying to you?" After they've had time to answer I move on to, "What did you do with what He said? Have you been obedient? How did you respond? What type of steps did you take?"

After working our way through these simple questions, nine times out of ten, we learn that their lack of response to what God spoke to them in the past has shown the Father they were not listening. If God associates hearing with doing, then we haven't heard until we've done. Let's say I asked Ella to clean her room. Even if she said, "Okay, Mom," I will assume I need to repeat myself until the evidence of a clean room shows up. Because the objective is for my children to listen to what I've ask them to do, I will not move onto the next thing until they've responded to the first thing.

Let's practice together. Answer the following questions.

What's the last thing you felt like the Father said to you?

_____

_____

_____

_____

Why do you think He might have said this to you?

_____

_____

_____

_____

How did you respond to what He said?

_____

_____

_____

_____

How did your response add or take away from the way you are currently hearing Him?

_____

_____

_____

_____

Is there an opportunity to go back to step one or even an opportunity to move to a new place of breakthrough? If so, what would that look like for you?

_____

_____

_____

_____

Repentance is best represented in turning around and walking a new direction. It's recognizing that, even though we might not be doing something wrong, God is doing something else and we want to be where He is. It's represented in letting go of whatever it is we currently cling to and opening our hands to what He has to offer. If repentance were sitting still then the opportunity for _bigger_ would be limited to where we are and what surrounds us. But because hearing means doing and repentance is shown in movement, _bigger_ is around every corner and opened to all possibilities.

Day 5—Challenge Day—Take the First Step

We spent all day yesterday talking about the things God has been saying to you, the invitations He might have placed before you and your decisions to join or not to join Him in His work. Today's your chance to take the step. We are actually all going to do it together. No more dilly-dallying. Today's the day. If you had a hard time coming up with one thing God is asking you to do then I want you to pause for a few minutes right here and ask Him to tell you something. If you already know what it was then skip to the next part.

Jeremiah 33:3 says, "Call to Me, and I will answer you. And I will show you great and wonderful things which you do not know."

God is waiting for your call, He has so much to tell you. After you've spent time calling to Him use the following prompts to better figure out your next move.

What I feel God inviting me to do is...

_____

_____

_____

_____

This invitation makes me feel...

_____

_____

_____

_____

This invitation would affect...

_____

_____

_____

_____

The length of time I've felt God inviting me into this is…

_____

_____

_____

_____

Some of the fruit that may come by accepting His invitation…

If doing implies hearing, then one thing I can do today to show that I've heard would be…

_____

_____

_____

_____

Okay, now go and do it. Don't allow the enemy to talk you out of it. We are going after *bigger* here and *bigger* lives just on the other side of broken. It doesn't matter how long it takes us to respond to Jesus, just that we respond. Your response to Him, shows you've heard and thus opens the line of communication between the two of you. It's highly likely you one step will lead to another and another and before you know it, you are on your ladder climbing towards *bigger*! Happy doing!

WEEK 5

SURRENDERING TO THE PROCESS
Book Chapters: 10-12

Small Group Discussion Guide

Repentance is hard. Changing direction takes guts. It's not easy to stop what you are doing (especially if it's a good thing) and join God on what He's doing. How have you turned around this week?

_____

_____

_____

Share with your group where you saw God at work?

_____

_____

_____

Were you able to find the strength to turn around and join Him where He was working? If so, what did that look like?

_____

_____

_____

Do you see your trust growing as you continue down this path of healing and redemption? If so, what are the ways you see this growth taking place?

_____

_____

_____

_____

How has your change in direction affected those around you?

_____

_____

_____

_____

Read Philippians 2:5-8. What picture of surrender does this paint for you?

_____

_____

_____

_____

Do you relate to the friction of wanting to surrender but fearing where surrender will lead you and the pain it may cause you?

_____

_____

_____

_____

Does it help to know Jesus struggled with this exact same thing?

_____

_____

_____

_____

Week 5—Personal Study Guide

We would never expect to build a house without any work. Building a house takes time, even when you hire a builder. There are plans to be drawn, decisions to be made and money to be spent. If we were freely given the opportunity to build the house of our dreams, we would take our time through every decision, making sure it was exactly what we wanted, being sure not to skip over any step. Everything would matter, even the minor details. Why would we assume our Father in Heaven, who knit us together, would do anything less? Our bodies, minds and lives reflect His masterful work. Every detail. He cares intently for each piece and what He rebuilds from our brokenness gets His best attention.

When we bought our last house it was bank-owned. I will never forget our first visit to the house that would soon become our home. What would have given nightmares to the average homebuyer was a dream come true to us. I'm lucky enough to be married to a rebuilder. Dave can see past the destruction of any home we stand in. No matter how bad off it may appear in the moment, he is gifted to paint a *bigger* picture. Because of his gift, we love the process of rebuilding. The idea of getting something with a good foundation, but still broken enough for no one to want it and pouring your own blood, sweat and tears (the tears from me because it never goes as planned!) is invigorating. The more we rebuild the more I love it. With each new house I understand a little more of the process. I fear a little less and we are a little more experienced. I'm not really interested in the perfect house someone else built anymore. I want one we can build together. I want our touch, our taste, and our style. I want to repaint, recarpet, refinish and rehabilitate the old, because those details matter to me.

Rebuilding from any type of brokenness always involves a process. *Bigger* is the promise, but we don't get there on accident. The work doesn't magically do itself. We don't turn around only to arrive at our final destination. Nehemiah heard from God. He recognized his place rebuilding the broken down walls of Jerusalem, but he still had to go. And even upon arrival I doubt he even had a clue of what the future really held. The first few work days may be hard and intimidating, but keep going. Take steps toward a *bigger* future. Believe in what He has told you and let Him have His way with you. Surrender is hard, but love lessens the blow. When you feel as though you can't let go of one more thing, remember how much you love Him. Remind yourself of all He has done for you. Go back to the table and rest in His presence. Feel His love and allow it to move you forward.

Day 1—The Beginning of Surrender

To throw your hands up in the middle of brokenness feels reckless. Not only does it feel reckless to you, it sometimes looks reckless to those watching. To some, surrender implies defeat. We've had it, given up, breathed our last breath, and purchased our last can of war paint. But to those who truly understand the secret of *bigger*, giving up is where it all begins.

The most reckless thing we do with our broken pieces is hold on to them. In our hands, they are only what they are, broken, shapeless, useless pieces. In His hands, they become the perfect materials for the *bigger* rebuilding process. The Webster definition of the word surrender is: *to agree to stop fighting, hiding, resisting, to give control or use of (something) to someone else.*

To surrender is to let go. It's to cease resisting. I can't tell you how many times I reluctantly drag my feet after repentance turns me around. It's not because I don't want to go. I've already repented. I've already decided where I was is not where I want to be, but still, something inside of me fears what I don't know.

Let's talk about surrender for a minute. Turn to 1 Samuel chapter 7 in your Bible. It's important you know a few details before we dive into this passage. The Israelites had been warring with the Philistines. In one such battle the Philistine Army defeated God's people and stole the Ark of the Covenant. The Ark of the Covenant represents the presence of God in the Old Testament. Wherever the Ark was, God's presence was there too. The Israelites, without the Ark, were destined for a life of defeat. The Philistines were winning until God showed up into the camp of the enemy. Each morning as the Philistine leaders went into their temple to worship their pagan god, they would find the Ark of the Covenant standing strong and the god of the Philistines, toppled over face down. Day after day it happened. And when that wasn't enough, the Philistine people began to break out in hives and sores all over their bodies. God was fighting for His people.

The Philistine leaders made up their mind. The Ark had to go. They packaged the Ark carefully, so as not to disrespect the one true God, and sent it back to their enemies, the Israelites. We pick up right as the Ark has arrived back into Israelite hands.

Please read 1 Samuel 7:1-2 and answer the following questions.

Where were the men who went to meet the Ark from?

_____

_____

_____

_____

Where did they take it?

_____

_____

_____

_____

Who was left in charge of it?

_____

_____

_____

_____

How long had the Ark been there?

_____

_____

_____

_____

What was going on in Israel during this time?

_____

_____

_____

_____

The men of Kiriath-Jearim received the Ark and took it to the hillside home of Abinadab. They ordained Eleazar, his son, to be in charge of it. For twenty years, the Ark remained in Kiriath-Jearim, but during this time all of Israel mourned and sought after the Lord because they felt abandoned by Him. They felt distant from Him, yet He was right there with them.

Is it possible to feel abandoned by God, when He is right in front of you?

_____

_____

_____

_____

Have you ever felt abandoned by God?

_____

_____

_____

_____

What were the events leading up to your abandoned feelings?

_____

_____

_____

_____

Thankfully, even when we are blind to see Him, God is not blind to see us. He is good to partner with other people in His pursuit of relationship. He loved the Israelites so much, He sent Samuel to help them. Is there someone in your life, who, when you struggle to recognize where God is, will help direct you back to Him? Who is this person and when was the last time they helped you? If you don't have this person in your life, does someone come to mind?

End your time today, thanking God for the Samuel in your life. If you are struggling to recognize where God is and what He might be doing, this might be a good time to reach out to your Samuel or to ask God to point you toward someone who could play this important role for you. Don't be like the Israelites mourning at the bottom of the hill for God. Look up and recognize He is right there.

Day 2—The Middle of Surrender

Samuel shows up on the scene and the Israelites are one big hot mess. It's a scary feeling to be disconnected from God, stumbling through life on your own. Especially when you know He is your only answer and a very real enemy lurks around every corner seeking to destroy you. The Israelites weren't just missing God, their Father. They were missing God, their Protector.

Read 1 Samuel 7:3-4.

What did Samuel tell the Israelites to do if they were really ready to return to the Lord with all their hearts?

_____

_____

_____

_____

Ashtoreth, or Asherah, was the name of the chief female deity worshiped in ancient Syria. Asherah was represented by a limbless tree trunk planted in the ground. The trunk was usually carved into a symbolic representation of the goddess. The Israelites were desperate for real interaction with God. They were missing their connection and because they refused to look up, they fell into the trap of idol worship.

Surrender, on ground level, with eyes stuck only on what we can see, is a nearly impossible task. The Israelites didn't want to create their own gods. They knew in their hearts there was more than this lowly place they currently existed. But, without looking up, they continued missing out. Their mourning after God showed how little satisfaction the pagan gods offered. There is never lasting joy when we delight ourselves in the lesser things of man.

Write Leviticus 26:1 below.

_____

_____

_____

_____

Now read Romans 1:18-23.

Who is Paul referring to in this passage?

_____

_____

_____

_____

Do these people know the truth about God? If so, how?

_____

_____

_____

_____

According to this passage, do you feel like there is a difference between knowing about God and knowing God? How would we be able to tell the difference?

_____

_____

_____

_____

What are some of these "idols" we see being worshiped in our culture today?

_____

_____

_____

_____

The idol worship has to stop so Samuel comes to them and says, "Listen, God is here. He has been here all along. You are the ones who haven't taken note. If you are ready to return to Him with ALL your heart, then get rid of all these false idols. Stop worshiping the gods in front of you and start worship the God above you. Look up! He knew with eyes fixed on all the things surrounding them, surrender was going to be impossible. But with eyes fixed above God's people would be free to lift their arms up," (1 Samuel 7:3, paraphrased).

Surrender is essential in the rebuilding process because only God has the master plans. Only He knows the *bigger* way to put the pieces back together. Only He sees how they fit. With our eyes down, we are easily tempted to believe we can figure it out. With eyes lifted up, focused on the Master Rebuilder, those details fade away as He steps in and recreates. Even after we've removed Band-Aids we sometimes continue holding on to the broken pieces in our lives. Surrender means no Band-Aids and no holding on. It's opening our hands to His work. Is it possible you are holding onto any broken pieces? What are those pieces?

_____

_____

_____

_____

Are you ready to lay them down? Are you ready to take your eyes off what's right in front of you and connect with what's above you? What does it look like for you to surrender to Him today? Is there something you need to let go of?

_____

_____

_____

_____

In the middle of our pain it's sometimes hard to see for the promises of God. Samuel was the eye God's people needed to reconnect with their one true love. Don't be afraid to tell someone you are having a hard time seeing. Healing doesn't happen in the dark. It happens out in the open, with the light of Christ shining all over us.

Write 2 Corinthians 12:9 below.

_____

_____

_____

_____

The middle of surrender is all about opening your hands. Will you open your hands and let go of the pieces you've previously clung to? Will you trust taking your eyes off what's in front of you will actually help you find the God above you? Will you find help to see what you cannot? Surrender won't accidentally happen. It is always a decision. Will you decide today?

Day 3—The End of Surrender

Start off reading 1 Samuel 7:4.

The Israelites burned their idols and returned to worshiping the one true God with all their hearts. It must have been a beautiful sight. For years, they walked around in depression, weeping and mourning after the God they were missing. With the help of Samuel, they were able to lift their heads up again. Their hope had been renewed.

When we connect with the One waiting to carry us forward the weight of going it alone lifts. I don't want to rain on the parade, because we should celebrate the initial surrender, but I also don't want to paint a false picture. If surrender is hard, then staying surrendered and living surrendered is harder. If we live this out correctly, the biggest battles we fight will always be on the inside. Our fight on the inside to surrender leaves Him fighting on the outside to bless.

God is good and faithful. He does not ask us to do something and then not reward us after we've obeyed. In the beginning it may feel like it doesn't even out, but in the end, our faithfulness to His promises always pay off. We are always left with more than we could ever hold.

Believing this truth will carry you through the process of surrender. Read 1 Samuel 7:5-13. Pay close attention to the sequence of events taking place after the Israelites burned their foreign gods and sought to serve the Lord only. Use the questions below to help piece together the story.

Where did Samuel send the Israelites?

_____

_____

_____

What did he plan to do for them there?

_____

_____

_____

Who caught wind of the Israelite surrender and movement?

_____

_____

_____

_____

What did the Philistine rulers prepare to do?

_____

_____

_____

_____

How did the Israelites respond (vs.7-8)?

_____

_____

_____

_____

How did God prove Himself faithful to the Israelites?

_____

_____

_____

_____

The enemy hates our surrender. He knows if he can keep our hands full of pieces, then we will never truly rebuild and with our eyes focused on what will never satisfy, we miss out on the *bigger* promises of God. With open hands and a head turned toward heaven, he panics. Brokenness placed in the trusted hands of the Master Rebuilder never come back less than *bigger*. God is the redeemer of all things broken and He never fails us.

We are most dangerous to the enemy with open hands. Thus the reason he rallies the troops to advance on us. If he can change our minds during those first initial moments of surrender, then he has a good chance of leading us right back to where we started.

Share about a time in your life when the enemy came hard after you as a direct result of your surrender.

_____

_____

_____

_____

_____

What the Israelites did in response to the advancement of the enemy is essential. They were already in prayer, confessing and repenting their sins. Even though the clanking of the enemy's armor approaching frightened them, they stayed focused. Instead of running back to their old ways, where they enemy would let them rest, the Israelites pleaded with Samuel to pray harder!

They knew their victory would come from God. They knew prayer was their most valuable weapon. They knew the Lord would answer them. Terrified, they called out to Him. Our most frightening moments should always drop us to our knees in prayer. On our knees, God is given the opportunity to fight the biggest battles for us.

Write Psalm 18:6.

_____

_____

_____

_____

_____

Write Psalm 145:18.

_____

_____

_____

_____

Write Philippians 4:6-7.

_____

_____

_____

_____

What is your initial response when you hear the enemy coming?

_____

_____

_____

_____

In what ways has your recent surrender gotten the attention of the enemy?

_____

_____

_____

_____

What kind of things is he using to cause you fear and doubt?

_____

_____

_____

_____

What do you feel God asking you to do today?

_____

_____

_____

_____

Sometimes my faith has to play catch up to my prayers. In other words, I'm praying for something and asking for the faith to believe in it all at the same time. The Israelites had no idea what to do. They were panicked, terrified and scared out of their minds. The enemy was coming, quickly. I become an easy target when my fear drives me to defend myself in a battle I wasn't meant to fight standing up.

Write Isaiah 41:10.

_____

_____

_____

_____

Now read John 14:27.

What does God promise to do for us when we call out to Him? What will He do with our fears?

_____

_____

_____

_____

God has big plans for the enemy. His plans always and only ever include the imminent defeat of the army of evil. There is nothing the enemy can do to overtake us if we are connected to the God of the universe. God did what the Israelites couldn't do. He got involved and He dealt with the enemy His way. I love it when God shows up and battles on our behalf. When our work is done in prayer, His work is done in full. The hardest battles we fight should be the battles we fight to let go and let God.

Day 4—A Lifetime of Surrender

Believe it or not surrender isn't a one-time thing. It would be nice if it was, wouldn't it? Because we walk in the flesh, we must continually resist the urges of the flesh. Paul knew what this continual life of surrender looked like and he wasn't afraid to hold the bar high for the rest of us.

Read Romans 7:15-20.

If you're like me, you might need to read it a few times, slowly, to really grasp what Paul was preaching! Even after making your way through this passage two or three times you may still be wondering what the heck Paul is trying to say. Have you ever been able to feel someone's pain even though you can't fully understand it? Obviously, Paul is struggling here. He's fed up with his flesh and the continual fight to surrender control of himself over to the Spirit.

Try reading it in the Message version, "I can anticipate the response that is coming: 'I know that all God's commands are spiritual, but I'm not. Isn't this also your experience?' Yes. I'm full of myself—after all, I've spent a long time in sin's prison. What I don't understand about myself is that I decide one way, but then I act another, doing things I absolutely despise. So if I can't be trusted to figure out what is best for myself and then do it, it becomes obvious that God's command is necessary. But I need something more! For if I know the law but still can't keep it, and if the power of sin within me keeps sabotaging my best intentions, I obviously need help! I realize that I don't have what it takes. I can will it, but I can't do it. I decide to do good, but I don't really do it; I decide not to do bad, but then I do it anyway. My decisions, such as they are, don't result in actions. Something has gone wrong deep within me and gets the better of me every time," (Rom 7:14-20 MSG).

It is absolutely impossible to live a life fully surrendered to God apart from the Holy Spirit. The Holy Spirit is the thread making it all possible. He is the piece inside us wooing our flesh more fully into submission. The Holy Spirit knows what our fleshly mind cannot understand; a life fully surrendered to the will of God is exactly where we want to be—even when it's hard, even when it doesn't make sense, even when it hurts.

Because of His divine connection with the Father, the Holy Spirit sees into the spiritual things we cannot always see. He works to open our ears to a language we don't fully understand. He is our direct connection to the Father.

Read John 14:15-21.

What does Jesus promise to his followers?

_____

_____

_____

_____

What kind of picture does the word *advocate* create for you?

_____

_____

_____

_____

Jesus knew His guys were going to freak a little when He told them He was leaving. But, He also knew they had no reason to panic because He and the Father had prepared a way. While in the presence of Jesus, the disciples knew what to do because they watched what Jesus was doing. Without Jesus, there would surely be a missing link. The Holy Spirit is our gift to fill in the gap. He is fully connected and fully aware of the heart of the Father and the call to *bigger*. He knows where we need to step and lays out the path to take us there.

Share a time where you have relied on the power of the Holy Spirit in you to do something through you, something you couldn't have done on your own.

_____

_____

_____

_____

The Holy Spirit is necessary as we move toward *bigger*. He steps in and does what we cannot do. We will never witness the rebuilding of ruins in our own strength. Not even Paul had what it took to win the battles in front of him independently. He needed help. Sometimes more help than he was comfortable needing. Some of us are really good help-givers, but really bad help-receivers. We are always there, on the front lines, fighting for those who need it. We are the funeral meal organizer, the last to go home after the church banquet and the loudest at the community rally, but when it comes to receiving we stiff-arm any help offered. The Truth of the Gospel is only ever received. What we give only comes from what we have first received. Meaning, if we haven't slowed down to receive, we don't have it to give. Nothing we have done or ever can do, will earn the amazing grace of the Gospel. The death of Jesus in our place is and always will be a freely given, undeserved gift. The very definition of grace is undeserved favor of God.

If everything in the Kingdom is received, then I need to become a good gift receiver. I need to welcome help. Needing help isn't a sign of weakness; it is actually a sign of strength. Brokenness always leads to *bigger* when placed in the hands of the Master Rebuilder.

When pride keeps us from receiving the help we need, it is our own strength blocking us from the *bigger* God has in mind. We cannot build lasting walls independently. We just can't. And once we partner with the Holy Spirit I'm not sure we ever want to do it on our own again.

Moses and the Israelites wandered through the desert for forty years. Talk about a process! *(Lord, please stop me before anything you're trying to teach me takes forty years of wandering!)* For years they fought to surrender and trust in God's promises over what was right in front of them. These people were so stubborn, even God grew impatient with them. They lived surrendered, un-surrendered, surrendered un-surrendered! It's exhausting to read much less live.

Everyone, except Moses. Moses lived a life of full surrender. It might have taken him a while to get to the point of total abandonment, but once he did there was no going back. He walked in obedient step with God. He knew if God told them there was an amazing life ahead, then they could trust there would be. He did not look at what was before him, instead he clung to what was above Him. He trusted *bigger.*

Read Exodus 33:1-6.

Where does God tell Moses to go?

_____

_____

_____

_____

What does God tell him them in verse 3?

_____

_____

_____

_____

Finally, the Israelites are going to cross into the Promised Land. After years of wandering and years of battling, they are on the edge of everything promised to them. The problem is their battle for surrender wasn't over yet. After all God had done for them, all He had shown them, they still clung to themselves.

Read Exodus 33:12-16.

What does Moses say to God?

_____

_____

_____

_____

Moses didn't care about the Promised Land if it cost him the promise of his relationship with the Father. His years of surrender left him completely dependent on God. He knew and trusted Him, more than even the good fruit of an abundant life. There is a point in our surrender when we consider it a privilege to open our hands unto the Lord. When we consider it an honor to sacrifice, to walk away, and to lay down our lives. The presence of God is a powerful thing. He is a force and experiencing Him in *bigger* ways always leaves us thirsty for more.

Write James 1:2-4 below.

_____

_____

_____

_____

When we trust *bigger* we consider it joy to be broken.

Day 5—Challenge Day—Helping Others in Surrender

Surrender is hard! It's not easy to lay down our idols and worship the Lord only. How hard has it been this week for you to turn your back on your idols? How many times did you second-guess your decision to trust God with everything even when you cannot see all the way around the corner?

Nehemiah walked away. His job for *the* king could not stand in the way of His job for *his* King. There is only room for one true God. Imagine how hard it was for Nehemiah to lay down everything, imagine the fear welling up inside of him, the anxiety. Approaching the King on behalf of the Israelites could have cost him his life. But God called him. And what God calls us to, He sees us through. If Nehemiah was supposed to rebuild the walls in Jerusalem, then he would rebuild the walls in Jerusalem. Just because he couldn't see his way around the corner didn't mean the plan was delayed. Would he serve God or would he serve his own purpose, identity and comfort?

One benefit of going through impossible surrender is it gives you compassion for others who are in the middle of surrender. Remember this feeling. It will come in handy the next time you are given the opportunity to encourage someone in the same place. Everyday, everywhere, people are being called to offer up more of themselves to the Living God. It's the ultimate calling on all of our lives. There is a great God before us, who has amazing things to accomplish both in and through our lives, but stepping fully into those destinies will cost us our entire lives.

The battle of surrender is a battle to give up your entire life. That's the end goal. Will you give Him absolutely everything? Because we also have a real life enemy, surrender is a never-ending battle. Don't let the reality of never-ending discourage you, the more we do it, the more we welcome it.

Think about the community you do life with. The people you interact with on a daily basis, maybe someone in your family, someone at work or even someone who attends your church and ask God to highlight the person He wants you to encourage today.

Once you have this person in mind spend a few minutes listening to God on his or her behalf. Ask God some of the questions below (you might want to write down anything you sense God saying to you so you can share it later). Make sure you are hearing the voice of a loving, encouraging Father and not your own voice or the voice of the enemy. One of the ways I check myself is through Scripture.

Ephesians 4:29 says, "Do not let any unwholesome talk come out of your mouths, but only what is helpful for building others up according to their needs, that it may benefit those who listen."

If God has told us to not let any unwholesome talk come out of our mouths and instead to only say what is helpful for building others up, then you can bet He will hold himself to the same standard. He is a good Father, always pointing people toward safety, always calling out the gold and always encouraging breakthrough. With that in mind, go through some of these questions on behalf of your person.

How do you feel about this person, Father?

_____

_____

_____

_____

_____

If you were sitting with them right now, what's one thing you would want to say to them?

_____

_____

_____

_____

_____

What hope and encouragement do you have for them concerning their future?

_____

_____

_____

_____

Spend a few minutes in prayer for this person and his or her future breakthrough.

_____

_____

_____

_____

Now is your chance to help someone in his or her surrender. I am thankful for the people in my life God sends to encourage me during those impossible moments. Their words are exactly what I need to take one more step forward. You might be that person to someone this week. Find a way to share your insight with the person you've talked with God about.

STEPPING ON YOUR LADDER
Book Chapters: 12

Small Group Discussion Guide

Think about the person God placed on your heart last week. What was his/her response to the encouragement you offered? Share with the group about your experience in taking a step of faith on behalf of someone else.

Where, in this journey, have you experienced the enemy trying to bring you down?

_____

_____

_____

_____

_____

_____

Coming out of surrender we usually have an opportunity for obedience. With newly open hands, we are able to grasp what it is God has in store for us. For Nehemiah it meant climbing on his ladder and getting to work. For us it might mean putting a pen to paper, starting a new ministry, calling up an old friend or some other form of stepping. Since you've opened your hands, have you felt Jesus trying to put anything in them? Is there a step He is asking you to take right now?

_____

_____

_____

_____

There is a time to rest and a time to work. It is in the balance of these two things we will arrive at *bigger.* We rest in the promises of who God is. We take time to sit down and hear Him in our brokenness. We grab for His outstretched arm and allow Him to pull us up. Then we start moving. We put our feet to the pavement and do the thing He's put in our heart to do. Do you see the step God might have in store for you?

_____

_____

_____

_____

What, if anything, about this step makes you hesitant? What makes you excited?

_____

_____

_____

_____

What might come out of your climb up the ladder?

_____

_____

_____

_____

Week 6—Personal Study Guide

Nehemiah's hardest work came in the secret place with the Father. If his fight to walk away from life as he knew it and surrender to bigger while battling to overcome the enemy and trusting God to rebuild what he couldn't fully see, then it's possible stepping on his ladder and doing the actual work felt easy.

When we spend the appropriate amount of time allowing God to do a work within us, allowing Him to do a work through us happens naturally. It should feel easy. Not easy, as in I don't have to do anything easy. But easy, as in the weight and pressure on my shoulders isn't there. When we deeply connect with the Spirit in the secret place and we carry His plans as we walk forward, then He carries the weight for us.

Inner work= hard
Outer work= easy

The problem is, most of the time, we want to skip the process and jump right on our ladders. We want instant - instant access, instant success and instant growth. I love homemade ice cream. Especially when my dad makes it. The kind you make on your own, not the Homemade brand. It's a process. You have to have all the right ingredients and then you have to tend to it, making sure the temperature is just right and the machine is churning at the correct speed. It's a lot of work, but the taste is off the charts. Experiencing real, homemade ice cream makes it hard to settle for the store bought kind. It taste false, not fresh. Something is missing. Something gets lost in the quickness of the process.

The same is true of our journeys. It is with time and preparation God brings forth abundant fruit in our lives. What would life look like if we stopped rushing to climb our ladders and surrendered to the slow process of transformation? What if we allowed each piece to be as important and necessary as He intended for it to be?

Nehemiah battled the enemy while he was on his ladder, but because God put him on the ladder, the enemy could not remove him. The taunting and lies never stood a chance. He wasn't shaken, wasn't moved and wasn't even swayed by outside influences.

Likewise, when God puts us on the ladder, no outside influence can bring us off. What He calls for, He provides for. He is the builder. He has the plans and when we trust Him enough not to get ahead of Him, He doesn't fail to come through for us. When we're on God-time, we actually gain time rather than lose it.

Day 1—The First Step Up

It would have appeared to the average American, Nehemiah wasted a lot of time. He spent days weeping, wailing and mourning over the brokenness before him. He spent valuable time waiting for the perfect moment to approach the king and then, even after he had everything he needed, he still kept quiet. He got out of bed in the middle of the night to secretly survey the land and gave God the space He wanted to download the right plan of action.

There is not much we wait for today. Let's be honest, if we want something, most of us go and get it. With instant access we have lost patience for process. We want our food fast, our time compensated and our cost minimal.

We get what we wait for.

If we skip over the process of spiritual formation and jump straight onto our ladders, then at some point we will fatigue and miss what lies ahead. David knew he would be the next king years before he ever sat on the throne. There was no instant ownership for this young anointed one. He didn't just have the promise of an ordained future; he had to carry the promise inside of him for an unknown amount of time while God worked.

What enables us to wait? How do we know when to step? What if we've stepped too soon? The process answers all of these questions and so many more. What is gained during our secret time with Jesus empowers us to do what we normally couldn't do. After spending an undefined amount of time in process, we will inevitably be given the opportunity to take our first step up the ladder toward *bigger*.

Up until this point, Nehemiah could throw in the towel and few people would notice. He could walk away and the Israelites would be unaware of the *bigger* rebuilding plans of their Father. But once he stepped out, God would step in and lives would be changed.

What God plants in secret, He means to bring forth in public. What are some of the *bigger* thoughts God has planted within you during your time in secret with Him?

_____

_____

_____

_____

_____

What practical steps could you take toward these *bigger* thoughts?

_____

_____

_____

_____

What scares you about these steps?

_____

_____

_____

_____

Stepping onto your ladder signifies it's time to work. God has done a work *in* you and now He wants to do a work *through* you. As we climb, He partners with us to bring His message of redemption and rebuild His Kingdom.

Knowing God differently enabled me to impact my community differently. In what ways have you come to know God differently?

_____

_____

_____

_____

How can this new found knowledge help you as you step on your ladder and point the way for others?

_____

_____

_____

_____

Read Romans 8:28.

How much of our life works out for good when given over to God?

_____

_____

_____

_____

What are some of the things you would have written off had it not been for God's redeeming power?

_____

_____

_____

_____

When stepping onto our ladders, what is the difference between someone who has been through the process of transformation and someone who hasn't?

_____

_____

_____

_____

At some point I made up my mind to trust God with my timing. Only He knows when we are ready and I was tired of always getting ahead of myself. Turning my clock of transformation over to Him has become a discipline I practice. I am committed to waiting for Him to do a work in me, instead of stepping prematurely into the work I want Him to do through me. The funny thing is, once He's done the work in me, the work through me seems to take care of itself. Why don't you give it a try? Where do you struggle with trusting God in your process of spiritual transformation? Would you benefit from pledging to Him a commitment to live on according to His watch instead of yours? Use the space below to craft a prayer committing yourself to His process of transformation. Pour your heart out to Him and trust His timing is always the best timing.

_____

_____

_____

_____

_____

_____

_____

_____

_____

_____

_____

_____

God intends for *bigger* to come from what is broken in our lives and He is willing to do a lot of work to get us there. Up until this point we have done a lot of seeking, sitting, praying, and preparing. Our ladder represents work. The desire for *bigger*, without the discipline to get there, doesn't amount to much. Rebuilding happens because God does what is necessary in us, and then we do what is necessary to move forward.

Nehemiah took many steps in preparation; now it was time to step up.

Day 2—Remember God

Allowing God to be Lord over our lives means we give Him full authority, full control, and full power to do what He wants, when He wants. It means recognizing we are no longer the authors of own stories. He is and we have accepted His invitation to play a role in the *bigger* stories He scripts.

Some of us will have an easier time remembering this than others. I have to remind myself of His authorship daily, because I prefer to hold the pen. The more I yield, the more I truly live. Living for Him brings satisfaction in ways I didn't realize possible. Living for myself never felt this good. To live for God means setting aside the things inside of us and going after a life totally free of self. It means wanting what He wants more than what we want.

I work hard to remind myself of who God is and what role I get to play in His story each day. Jesus also worked hard to remind himself who his Father was. Read Matthew 26:39. In what way is Jesus remembering the task given to Him?

_____

_____

_____

_____

What does Philippians 2:5-8 tell us about the mindset of Jesus?

_____

_____

_____

_____

Do you think remembering God and having this mindset strengthened or weakened Jesus when it came to finishing the task He was sent to do?

I love the part in Philippians where it says, "He made himself humble," (Phil 2:7 NIV.) Jesus chose humility. Climbing the corporate ladder often brings up thoughts of self-preservation and promotion. It's that whole *do whatever it takes to get ahead,* mindset. But climbing the ladder toward *bigger* actually means humbly doing what others won't. It means putting them first, even the ones who also put themselves first. If we look at the life of Jesus, the climb toward *bigger* is actually represented in sacrifice, servanthood, surrender and even death. It's putting everyone before you.

God is sovereign. His sovereignty gives Him supreme rule and power of all. If we trust in His sovereignty then we don't have to fear our climb to *bigger*. This trust is the very reason why the secret place and spiritual transformation are necessary. Without it we will, no doubt, retreat and take the climb into our own hands. On our own we may get higher, but we will never arrive at the *bigger* God intended.

Let's study about the sovereignty of God. What do all of these verses teach you about God and His rule?

Read Psalm 115:3. What does it tell you about God?

_____

_____

_____

_____

What about Job 42:4?

_____

_____

_____

_____

Proverbs 19:21
What is Romans 9:19-21 saying about the potter and the clay?

_____

_____

_____

_____

_____

_____

_____

_____

_____

_____

_____

_____

_____

_____

And finally, Ephesians 2:10.

_____

_____

_____

_____

What does your life teach others about God and His rule?

_____

_____

_____

_____

If God is in charge, then let Him be in charge. If we trust Him, then let's really trust Him. No more pretending. Step on your ladder and remember who He is. Remembering God will enable you to climb against all odds, in the strangest circumstances and through the strongest winds.

Day 3—Remember Your People

God is highly relational. He always chooses relationship. It's what He does. It's who He is. If He weren't so stuck on relationship, then He would simply do this whole big thing without us. He doesn't need us. He wants us! The fact that we are created in His imagine means we are highly relational also. Even introverts need relationship to exist. No one is meant to travel alone. Because of relationship our pursuit of the *bigger* things of God affects others. What I do for Jesus will impact what my kids do for Jesus. It will impact what my friends do for Jesus, what my family does and will even impact people I don't know. My pursuit of Him should affect my friends, my family and my community. If I really chase after Him other people are going to notice. The day my faith in Jesus doesn't get the attention of those near me is the day I need to sit down and reevaluate my tactics.

Other people should notice when you follow Jesus to *bigger*.

God began to build something inside Nehemiah. The work He was doing empowered Nehemiah to walk away from His job and forward into the unknown. For a while, this work was personal and private, but as Nehemiah traveled further down the road, God put him out among people for the work. We don't build alone because building alone is dangerous.

Read about the events and the morale unfolding mid-way through the build in Nehemiah 4:10-23. What's happening to the workers?

_____

_____

_____

_____

What do they say to Nehemiah?

_____

_____

_____

_____

They were ready to give up. Rebuilding this massive wall was taking a toll on their health and their families. There was no end in sight and they were beginning to think life was better off broken. Have you ever been there? You are mid-way through the process and wondering if things were better off the way they used to be.

When you found yourself in this place, what did you do? Did you quit and go back? Why or why not?

_____

_____

_____

_____

Thankfully, Nehemiah knew the secret: *Remember.*
What does he tell them in verse 14?

_____

_____

_____

_____

After they remembered the Lord, who were they supposed to remember next?

_____

_____

_____

_____

Isn't it funny how sometimes all we have to do to keep going is remember who is working alongside us? You have people with you, but you must discipline yourself to look up from your work and remember them. Nehemiah called them to remember their families back home. The ones they were fighting for. He also called them to spread themselves out more. Half of the men were called to be on ladders, building, and the other half were down below standing guard. Everyone had a place and every place was essential for the protection of the kingdom.

Who do you have on a ladder, building beside you?

_____

_____

_____

_____

What support can you gain from this relationship?

_____

_____

_____

_____

Read Ecclesiastes 4:9-12. What does this say about the need for more than one person to travel with through life?

_____

_____

_____

_____

With two or more you have protection. Nehemiah knew it was wise to put multiple rebuilders on their ladders. He also knew it was wise to have guards at the bottom of those ladders keeping watch for movements from the enemy. It would be very hard to defend yourself while on top of a ladder.

Have you felt the intense attack of the enemy as you climbed toward *bigger*? How did you fight back?

_____

_____

_____

_____

Ladders are interesting things. They provide support to get us to higher ground, but they are susceptible to the elements around them. Have you ever tried to use a ladder on uneven ground? It's a very difficult process. The other day, my husband, Dave, used a pressure washer to clean the side of our house. Our house sits on a hill, which made the task extra difficult when he needed the ladder. My job, at the bottom of the ladder was to steady it as he worked.

Read 2 Corinthians 7:5-7. What was going on with Paul? Who did God choose to speak through?

_____

_____

_____

_____

Titus was exactly the motivation Paul needed to keep climbing. He was the encouragement; he was the strength. He was the person also climbing and willing to reach out to steady Paul's ladder when necessary. We need others. My story is your story because our stories together make up part of God's story.

Who is at the bottom of your ladder that will reach out and steady you when you begin to wobble?

_____

_____

_____

_____

If you are unsure who this person is, spend some time today asking God to open your eyes. If you have in any way grown distant from this person, spend your time today reaching out once again and inviting them back into this journey. Don't climb alone. It's far too dangerous.

Day 4—Remember the *bigger*

Though the *bigger* things of God and the process of getting there may be overwhelming for us, it doesn't overwhelm God. He isn't worried. He trusts the process and He values each and every piece. God will never let you down; He will never let you be pushed past His limit because He doesn't have one. He will always be there in our weakness to provide the strength necessary to continue. Life is going to be hard and at times overwhelming. There will be days when the cost seems too high. Even on those days, His promises remain true.

Read Romans 8:28-29.

I love how it is written in the Message version, "Meanwhile, the moment we get tired in the waiting, God's Spirit is right alongside helping us along. If we don't know how or what to pray, it doesn't matter. He does our praying in and for us, making prayer out of our wordless sighs, our aching groans. He knows us far better than we know ourselves, knows our pregnant condition, and keeps us present before God. That's why we can be so sure that every detail in our lives of love for God is worked into something good" (Rom. 8:28–29 MSG).

Have you ever found yourself in a situation so unfamiliar that you didn't know what or how to pray? What did you do?

_____

_____

_____

_____

_____

_____

I remember the tragic death of a loved one hitting me so suddenly I couldn't speak. I didn't have words *(I know, hard to imagine, right!)*. In those moments the worst thing we can do is pressure ourselves to pray wordy prayers. Talk about disconnecting from the healing God wants to provide us. Focusing on ourselves always leaves us short. God doesn't need your words, He only needs your heart, whether it's full, bursting, broken or completely shattered. During those intense moments we must train our minds to remember the *bigger* He has promised from the broken.

Write out Isaiah 55:8-9 below.

_____

_____

_____

_____

Be honest about something in your life you don't understand. Write the circumstance below.

_____

_____

_____

_____

Now be honest with God in prayer. If you have words, pray them. If you don't, sit in front of Him on behalf of this situation and let Him pray for you. The Holy Spirit will do the work, you just focus on being still and clearing your mind. God knows what you don't. If you trust in Him and you trust in His process of rebuilding, then you can trust He will not leave you here in this unexpected pain.

Do you remember what we learned about where God is in relationship to the brokenhearted? Reread Psalm 34:18 from one of our earlier weeks. If we want to be near God, where is the best place to find Him?

_____

_____

_____

_____

**Remembering the _bigger_ means trusting
where there is brokenness, there is God.**

Day 5—Challenge Day—Steadying Ladders

Sometimes we are on the ladder and other times we work to steady the ladders of those in community with us. Today's a good day to steady a few ladders. Think about your community. Who are the people in your life chasing Jesus with you? What brokenness are they currently rebuilding? Where could they use a little encouragement concerning the climb ahead of them? Have any of them come down off of their ladder and gone back to the comfort of brokenness?

Spend your time out today encouraging those around you. Ask God to give you eyes to see what He sees. Ask Him to strengthen your hands for the work ahead. God is so multifaceted, we can climb our own ladders, putting into practice the things God has spoken over us in the secret place, all the while steadying the ladder of those around us.

Before you pray today consider some of these questions.

Who in your community might be struggling to climb his or her ladder?

_____

_____

_____

_____

Why do you think God might have brought this person(s) to your attention today?

_____

_____

_____

_____

Do you know of a practical way to steady his or her ladder?

_____

_____

_____

_____

Now spend the remainder of your time in prayer for this person(s). Once you finish, get to work!

WEEK 7

OVERCOMING THE ENEMIES CHATTER
Book Chapter: 13

⊢————————————⊣

Small Group Discussion Guide

How's it going on your ladder? Share with your group one small step you took this week toward *bigger*.

_____

_____

_____

_____

In what ways were you able to reach out and steady the ladder of someone climbing beside you?

_____

_____

_____

_____

How are you feeling on your climb? Is your ladder wobbling? A little? A lot? What do you think is making it so shaky?

_____

_____

_____

In what ways do you tend to notice the attack of the enemy concerning your life personally? Do you think he might have stepped up his game since you climbed on your ladder?

_____

_____

_____

_____

_____

Read Ephesians 6:10-18 and discuss the following questions.
What kind of battle are we fighting?

_____

_____

_____

_____

What are the different types of armor we have been given?

_____

_____

_____

_____

What is the one weapon we hold?

_____

_____

_____

_____

How good are you at using this weapon?

_____

_____

_____

_____

How well do you walk in your armor?

_____

_____

_____

There are some days I forget to even put mine on. Those are the days the enemy seems to be around every corner, hidden in every conversation, mocking me with every decision. Sometimes it's as simple as making the daily decision to suit up rather than go at it unprepared.

What might you need to change to ensure you suited yourself for battle each day?

Week 7—Personal Study Guide

Nehemiah walked away from his job, his title, his security, and his entire life. God confirmed his faithful decision by moving the King of Susa to provide him with assistance. A full caravan of help accompanied Nehemiah into Jerusalem. Imagine the feelings in the pit of their stomachs upon first glance of the broken down mess that used to be a protective wall. Nehemiah had an impossible job to do. Luckily, he served a God of the impossible. Interrupted by his heartbreak over the broken state of his people, Nehemiah made a new home for himself in Jerusalem.

"I went to Jerusalem, and after staying there three days, I set out during the night with a few others. I had not told anyone what my God put in my heart to do for Jerusalem. There were no mounts with me except the one I was riding on. By night I went out through the Valley Gate toward the Jackal Well and the Dung Gate, examining the walls of Jerusalem, which had been broken down, and its gates, which had been destroyed by fire. Then I moved on toward the Fountain Gate and the King's Pool, but there was not enough room for my mount to get through; so I went up the valley by night, examining the wall. Finally, I turned back and reentered through the Valley Gate. The officials did not know where I had gone or what I was doing, because as yet I had said nothing to the Jews or the priests or nobles or officials or any others who would be doing the work," (Nehemiah 2:11-16).

Three days after settling into his new home, Nehemiah rose in the middle of the night and made his way through the beloved city of his ancestors. He took careful notes of each gate, trying to discern where the work needed to start. Nehemiah did it in secret so as to not cause any alarm or unnecessary concern amongst God's people. Not knowing what his first move would be, there was no need to bring on premature emotions.

Nehemiah knew God would reveal the plan for *bigger*, He just needed time. In secret God and Nehemiah surveyed the land. In secret they built the plans. In secret they charted their mission. Some of the greatest work we will do with the Father will be the work we do in secret, planning and preparing for the tasks ahead. The harder we work in the secret place, the harder He works in the public place. Because Nehemiah heard God's voice in the secret place, He was able to fight the enemy in the public place. No way was he backing off now. He had come to far. God had done a mighty work within him. His heard was involved. It was broken. Broken enough to walk away from His job, his community, his security and his comfort. He was in now, right in the thick of it. The enemy could do whatever He wanted because Nehemiah wasn't listening.

We have a real enemy and he is really good at getting inside our heads, if we let him. It's best to remind ourselves ahead of time of the enemies desire to steal, kill and destroy (John 10:10.) Sometimes we get caught off guard simply because we've forgotten to remember. Nehemiah couldn't risk forgetting. Neither can we. Don't forget we have an enemy who is out to get us.

Day 1—The Real Battle

Nehemiah made his plan. He rallied the troops. He shared about what God brought him to do and charged them with an opportunity to participate in one of the greatest rebuilding projects in the entire Bible.

Read Nehemiah 2:17-18.

How did the people respond to Nehemiah?

_____

_____

_____

They were ready. Tired of being defined and controlled by the brokenness they used to call home, they strapped on their working boots, dug out their old ladders and showed up ready to build. As soon as the work on the wall started, the enemy outside the wall, noticed. A rebuilt wall meant stability for God's people. The enemies surrounding the great wall preyed upon the broken circumstances of God's people. Without a wall, Israel was unable to fend them off. They were victims. With repair work beginning, the enemies rallied together. A rebuilt wall for the Israelites, meant less control for them.

We have a real life enemy who pays careful attention when God steps into our lives with fresh rebuilding plans. He knows brokenness in *our* hands is nothing to worry about, but brokenness in *His* hands takes on new meaning. What He builds never falls. The enemy is present as we weep, he is there as we start to stand, he is watching as we hesitantly follow God out of brokenness, but when we pull our ladder up to the wall and start to work, He gets up. There is no way, will he sit idly by while we climb to new heights with the Ultimate Rebuilder. He will do whatever it takes to get our eyes back to those helpless, broken pieces.

Read Ephesians 6:10-12. You read this during your group time. Let's dive a little deeper into it today.

Against whose schemes are we to stand?

_____

_____

_____

What does it mean that our struggle is not against flesh and blood?

_____

_____

_____

_____

How do you typically fight the enemy in your life?

_____

_____

_____

_____

More times than not, I think fighting a physical battle would be easier than fighting the spiritual battles we encounter every day. Nothing feels better to me than a long run after a hard day. Being able to run off frustration and sweat out failure is so healthy. Unfortunately the spiritual battles we fight are much different. These battles don't play by the same rules. We battle an unseen enemy over control of very real emotions. Our enemy fights to oppress and distract us. With each step, our attention to the *bigger* leaves him fuming in defeat. He will use any means possible to keep us from reaching our fullest potential in Christ.

Because of their sheer power to control our actions, our minds are often the first place of attack. Nehemiah was fighting a real enemy. What he battled in the physical, he would also battle in the spiritual.

Write John 8:44 below.

_____

_____

_____

_____

The enemy is a liar. Therefore, we must train ourselves to recognize when his deceiving ways are before us. "The weapons we fight with are not the weapons of the world. On the contrary, they have divine power to demolish strongholds. We demolish arguments and every pretension that sets itself up against the knowledge of God, and we take captive every thought to make it obedient to Christ" (2 Cor. 10:4–5).

A good way to define the word stronghold is this: anything, other than God, that has a strong hold on us. There is but one person capable of giving us the life we desire. Looking to or depending on anything else crosses over into enemy territory.

Thinking back over your journey up to this point, can you recognize any places where you might have a stronghold?

_____

_____

_____

_____

Use the space below to ask God to speak to you about this particular stronghold. Where might it have come from? What might the root be? The first step in tearing down our strongholds is learning to recognize why we have them.

_____

_____

_____

_____

_____

_____

_____

_____

_____

_____

_____

_____

_____

Day 2—Recognizing the Enemy

Part of the problem with the enemy is, he doesn't show up dressed like the enemy. Write 1 Peter 5:8.

_____

_____

_____

_____

_____

_____

Lions looking to attack get low to the ground. They quickly and quietly stalk the unsuspecting animal. And then, with their heart pounding with anticipation of their next catch, they pounce taking the innocent victim by surprise. We cannot expect to battle the enemy if we do not first train ourselves to recognize him. He is sneaky and good at what he does. He is quietly watching us and waiting for the perfect time to pounce and catch us off guard.

A good friend of mine was once a bank teller. As a part of her job she spent hours studying the look and feel of real bills. Her job was to know money so well, when counterfeit money came across her counter, it would instantly stand out to her. Think about it: there are thousands of counterfeit bills. They all look different, similar to the real bill in most ways, but each one of them is unauthentic in its own way. Learning to recognize every counterfeit bill would be impossible. The banks are on to something. Training people to know the real bills, inside and out, is the best way to protect against the crime of counterfeit money.

We have an enemy intent on stealing, killing and destroying all hope of rebuilding. He will take any form necessary to keep us sitting in our brokenness. He has no shame and will even use the things most precious to us to remove our hope of restoration. The best way to fight the enemy is to know and understand the voice of the Father so well that when a counterfeit voice or thought comes through our mind, it stands out quickly and loudly.

How good are you at recognizing the difference between the voice of God and the voice of the enemy?

_____

_____

_____

_____

When the enemy comes at our minds we have to recognize Him. The best way to know the difference is to *know* the real deal. The Hebrew word for *KNOW* in the Old Testament is *Yada*. *Yada* doesn't just mean to *know of*, like, *I know Ella doesn't like the color red*. It means to *know intimately*, know inside and out, know personally. For example, *I know Ella wants to be a dancer when she grows up. She spends hours in her room practicing. Her favorite type of dance is lyrical. She is an amazing storyteller on the dance floor. When she dances her passion and love ooze out of her.*

Genesis 4:1 in our King James Version says, "Adam knew Eve his wife." The Hebrew word *yada* means "Adam yada'd Eve." He knew her, intimately, sexually, physically, and emotionally. He knew what she felt like, what she smelled like. He knew her disposition. Her quirks. He even recognized her giggle. He knew her. Better than anything or anyone.

We were created to *yada* God. To know Him, intimately. We were designed for Him to complete us. Knowing God intimately is what helps us recognize Him. Think about a loved one. Someone you know so intimately you could close your eyes and find them in a crowded room simply by the sound of their laugh. Knowing God this way enables us to battle the enemy. Knowing God this way gives us the victory we have been promised.

What do the following Scriptures promise? Remember as you read the word *know*, you are really reading the word *"yada."*

Psalm 9:10

_____

_____

_____

_____

Psalm 16:11

_____

_____

_____

_____

Jeremiah 1:5-6

_____

_____

_____

_____

John 8:32

_____

_____

_____

_____

Knowing God changes everything, but it takes time to know someone intimately. If we are going to best equip ourselves to recognize the enemy, then we must spend an adequate amount of our time coming to know the authentic God. He is the One who will lead us to *bigger*. He is the One with the redeeming plans. He is the One capable of making all things new. The secret place is where this love is fostered. It's where it grows. When you give yourself the space to be alone with Him you get to know Him on an entirely new level.

On a scale of 1-10 (10 being the highest, 1 being not at all) how well would you say you currently know the Father?

_____

_____

_____

_____

Would you be able to pick out His voice in a crowded room? When is the last time you noticed Him speaking over the noise?

_____

_____

_____

_____

Is there a time or place where you hear His voice best?

_____

_____

_____

_____

My prayer is that throughout the course of this Bible study you have fallen a little more in love with His voice. In secret Nehemiah walked the property, surveyed the land and constructed the plans for the massive rebuilding project in front of Him. If Nehemiah needed time alone with God to understand his next step, how much more do we? Our time with Him doesn't end just because we step on our ladder. It's needed even more now as we climb toward *bigger* and battle a real life enemy who will stop at nothing to bring us down.

Day 3—Resisting the Enemy

The chatter of the enemy grew a little louder with each passing day of work.

Read Nehemiah 2:19.

Who was it laughing at Nehemiah?

_____

_____

_____

_____

What were they saying?

_____

_____

_____

_____

Sarcasm is a powerful tool. I spent much of my teenage years in my room because of it! The enemy used sarcasm as a weapon to create fear and doubt amongst the people. Sanballat, was the leader of the Samaritans and had been using his position of power to subdue God's people. Nehemiah's sudden interest in rebuilding the wall put a damper on Sanballat's access to the vulnerable Israelites. He didn't wait long to show up. Nehemiah barely began his work and Sanballat's sarcastic words began ringing in his ears.

Read Nehemiah 2:20 and note Nehemiah's response to his enemy.

I'm not worried. God will supply all we need. With that said, he went back to work. We give the enemy too much of our time. His words are not powerful enough to withstand even the smallest thing God has put into motion. According to James 4:7, all we have to do is resist him and he will run from us. We need to learn to not waste unnecessary time battling. Speak it and be done with it. Tell him to leave and move forward without him.

Write James 4:7 below.

_____

_____

_____

Think for a minute about the word resistance. When I think of that word I picture those deceiving colored resistance bands tucked in a corner of my workout room. They might look all nice and comfortable over there in the corner, but add them into a workout and comfort goes out the window. Resistance is hard, even when we are sitting still. Working through resistance is even harder! Though it is hard, it is also necessary if you want to build muscle mass. The best muscles are built in resistance. Nehemiah worked, he resisted and he built the muscles necessary for the climb to *bigger*. For the next two chapters, Nehemiah pressed on and continued his work. The sarcastic chatter of the enemy was heard, but not as loudly as the clanging of the hammers beating on the wall.

Read Nehemiah 4:1-3. Who is talking again? What is he saying this time?

_____

_____

_____

_____

Read Nehemiah 4:4. What was the response of the Israelites?

_____

_____

_____

_____

Nehemiah 4:6 says they rebuilt the wall until it was half its original height. Not bad for a couple week's work. These guys were on a roll. Working, resisting, sleeping, working, resisting, sleeping. Their hard work was paying off and the enemy once again took note.

This time Sanballat came at them with a different tactic. Maybe the thought of a physical attack would bring these rehabbers down off of their ladders. To prepare for an impending attack the Israelites positioned their troops and Nehemiah readjusted their plans. Read Nehemiah 4:13-23 and explain Nehemiah's battle plan.

Nehemiah positioned workers and warriors. Some men worked, other men stood guard, each an essential piece of the rebuilding. We need protectors all around us as we work to rebuild the ruins in our lives. Those protectors could see what the workers couldn't. They stood watch over their friends laboring on their ladders. It's a beautiful picture of family. We are better together, watching each other's backs and fighting for *bigger.*

Who has your back? Do you have people in your life standing guard as you battle to rebuild the ruins? Sometimes in our brokenness shame leaves us trying to rebuild on our own. Resistance is harder alone. We were meant to battle together, to strengthen one another. Don't make it harder than it has to be by trying to go it alone. It might be time for you to step out and invite someone in on your battle.

Sanballat's final attack was a sneaky one. It actually came from within. Read Nehemiah 6:1-2. What did Sanballat try to do?

_____

_____

_____

_____

When everything else backfired, Sanballat thought he would take a swing and pretend to be on Nehemiah's side. If *you can't beat 'em, join 'em, right?* Never is it more important to know the voice of your Father than when your work of resistance has taken you almost to the top of your ladder. The enemy is sly, he delights in adding chaos and confusion to the project and he will pretend to be your friend if that's what it takes to bring you down.

The most clear cut example I can think of for this in my life came my freshman year in college. Playing college soccer was on the top of my list. However, with such a new faith, I knew it would be nearly impossible for me to play college soccer and grow in my relationship with Jesus. We were rebuilding through a lot of brokenness and I felt confirmed Jesus was asking me to put this dream on hold and focus on rebuilding. My new faith was too important. I nervously turned down a really nice scholarship to a school in Kentucky and finalized all my paperwork to attend Miami University of Ohio. There, I would be close to home and the people be encouraging me in this new journey. Two weeks into my time at Miami, someone approached me about playing soccer for the school club team. It was a great invitation. A club team wouldn't keep me away as much. It wouldn't be as demanding and surely I could handle this. Even though something inside of me wasn't feeling right, I went to the first day of try-outs and nailed it. Which got me invited back for the second day. I was up all night, tossing and turning. My stomach in knots. Something inside of me still knew this wasn't the answer. The voice of the enemy came through opportunity. God was building something new in me and in order to do it He needed my full attention. He had already told me this, why would He change His mind? Thankfully because I knew the Lord and was already working to rebuild my life with Him, I was able to resist the enemy's last ditch effort to distract me.

In what ways have you noticed the enemy trying to distract and destroy the work you've done so far?

_____

_____

_____

_____

I love Nehemiah 6:9, "But I prayed, "Now strengthen my hands."

Do you need to ask for stronger hands? If so, pray this with me: *Heavenly Father, strengthen our hands. Steady our work. Focus our eyes. Enable us to resist the efforts of the enemy. Keep us focused on the task ahead of us. Position us with people who will stand guard on our behalf and empower us to obtain the bigger.*

Day 4—Replacing the Enemy

What we put into our minds makes a difference. You don't have to spend long at any gym to find the "serious" ones. Those muscle-loaded guys and girls walking around lifting more with one hand then you and your jogging partner's weight put together. Have you ever paid attention to what these fitness gurus do when their workout ends? A lot of times the first thing they do upon finishing a workout is guzzle this chalky looking drink mix. Kudos to them! I tried it once. For about a week. I couldn't stomach it any longer. I'm clearly not cut out to be a body-builder. If I'm going to drink a protein shake, then I need my blender and some flavor and maybe even a little chocolate!

But let me tell you about this process. It's so interesting when you parallel it to the process of fighting off the enemy. This protein drink does so much for the production of our muscles. When we lift weights the strain of lifting tears our muscle fibers. These tiny tears are essentially what enhance and grow the muscle in the long run, but what we put into our bodies between workouts aids in the healing process. Without an adequate amount of protein our muscles can't heal as quickly, which can lead to overtraining and injury.

When a workout is finished and proteins enter the body, they make their way to the site of strain and tear and replenish what has been depleted. In the long run the muscle fibers are repaired and restored to be stronger and even more effective than they were before.

Spiritually, when we recognize and refuse the enemy we are opening ourselves up and using stored energy. What we put in our minds after these intense battles works to replenish and protect us. Addilyn, my youngest, is a soccer player. She loves everything about soccer and I couldn't be happier about being a soccer mom. But, early on, she had to learn the basics. Practicing in our yard, I taught her how to kick the ball. Over and over again, I repeated to her, "Don't use your toe, Addy. Don't use your toe."

What happens if I never replace the wrong behavior with the right one? Addilyn would know how to *not* kick the ball, but she still wouldn't know how to actually kick the ball. With our faith, we cannot only focus on the wrong things. We have to spend time refueling ourselves with the right things. We grow better at resistance when we refuel with the proper nutrients.

Let's practice together for a minute. What's one lie the enemy has spoken to you in the past week? (I will do this part with you to set an example.)

This past week the enemy tried to convince me I should be worried about the future.

How did you recognize this wasn't the voice of God?

I recognized it wasn't the voice of God because I know God tells me over and over again in His Word not to worry about my future. He wouldn't tell me one thing in His Word and another thing in my mind. If He said it, He meant it.

Once you recognized this lie, what did you do to refuse it?

In order to refuse the lie, I stood up, took a deep breath and told myself this wasn't the truth. The feeling I had inside of me wasn't from God. What was going through my mind did not represent the mind of Christ and therefore; I did not have to think it either. I resisted it. Over and over.

Now that you have recognized the lie and resisted it, what are you going to replace the lie with?

I am going to replace the lie with this passage. Each time the enemy tries to use this lie against me, I am going to remember what this passage says and speak it as Truth for my life and my future.

Matthew 6:25, "Therefore I tell you, do not worry about your life, what you will eat or drink; or about your body, what you will wear. Is not life more important than food, and the body more important than clothes? Look at the birds of the air; they do not sow or reap or store away in barns, and yet your heavenly Father feeds them. Are you not much more valuable than they? Who of you by worrying can add a single hour to his life? And why do you worry about clothes? See how the lilies of the field grow. They do not labor or spin. Yet I tell you that not even Solomon in all his splendor was dressed like one of these. If that is how God clothes the grass of the field, which is here today and tomorrow is thrown into the fire, will he not much more clothe you, O you of little faith? So do not worry, saying, What shall we eat? or What shall we drink? or 'What shall we wear? For the pagans run after all these things, and your heavenly Father knows that you need them. But seek first his kingdom and his righteousness, and all these things will be given to you as well. Therefore do not worry about tomorrow, for tomorrow will worry about itself. Each day has enough trouble of its own."

Now it's your turn.

What is one lie the enemy has tried to sneak by you this week?

_____

_____

_____

_____

How did you recognize it was the voice of the enemy and not the voice of God?

_____

_____

_____

_____

Once you recognized this lie, what did you do to resist it?

_____

_____

_____

_____

Now that you have recognized the lie and resisted it, what are you going to replace the lie with? *(This is the part where you might have to do a little research. If you don't know a Scripture to fight back with right away, that's okay. But make time to find one. You can use the back of most Bibles or you can even go on multiple Bible programs and search by topics for related Scripture. The more you learn Scripture, the quicker you become at replacing the lies with Truth.)*

If you find yourself having a hard time replacing the lies, try replacing some of the things surrounding you. Think about what you listen to, what you read, the conversations you have, the places you go. The things you take in have to be processed somewhere. What are some of the things you spend your time doing that might be enabling this lie?

_____

_____

_____

_____

Write Matthew 5:29 below.

_____

_____

_____

_____

Jesus' words here are pretty extreme. I think He means, if that book makes it hard for you to be married to your husband, stop reading it; even better, throw it away so no one reads it. If that show makes you want what you cannot afford, turn it off. If that friend entices you to fall into sin you have sworn off limits, find a new friend.

As much as we wish the old saying to be true, things rarely go in one ear and out the other. Participating in the *bigger* purposes of God is a privilege. This privilege comes with great responsibility. God will continue to show up and blow your mind with what He does in your life, if you will continue to be responsible with what you look at and listen to.

Change the way you think and it will change the way you act. Be protective of the things you take in. Take in things leading you to *bigger*.

Day 5—Challenge Day—Take Back Your Ground

Gaining back our ground is as simple and as hard as surrender. Our victory will come only when we actually throw our hands up in defeat. That's because the battle has already been fought and the victory already accomplished. We don't have to worry who wins in the end. We simply have to be willing to keep walking forward. God's plans never include us sitting in defeat.

Are there areas of your life where the enemy is holding you back? What are those areas?

_____

_____

_____

_____

Can you recognize the lies keeping you still? If so, list some of them below.

_____

_____

_____

_____

I want you to spend your time today practicing.

Recognize who is speaking to you.
Refuse and resist the voice and power of the enemy in your life.
Replace it with the Truth of God.

It might look like this: *I recognize my diet is an area of defeat in my life. I think I need things I really don't need and when I eat them they leave me feeling less satisfied than I was before eating them. The truth is, I don't have to be dependent on anything other than Jesus. It doesn't make me feel better, it makes me feel worse and I don't need it. I'm going to replace it with those words but also by removing the temptations out of my pantry and changing my grocery list to reflect a grocery list which will enable me to be the person God has called me to be.*

Or this: *I recognize my husband seems stressed. He is short with the kids, even shorter with me and distracted while he is at home. I want to lash out and help him see how unfair it is for him to take his stress out on his family. But that would only make him feel worse. The Truth in Proverbs 15:1 reminds me, "a gentle answer turns away wrath, but a harsh word stirs up anger. I am going to resist the enemy telling me I need to fight back and lash out and instead I am going to speak gently and softly. I will take my concerns to God and trust He will speak on my behalf.*

Okay, it's your turn. Recognize the lies, resist them and then take the physical step today of replacing and moving into the place of victory. Use the space below to write out your action plan.

_____

_____

_____

_____

WEEK 8

DREAMING BIGGER
Book Chapters: 14-17

$\longmapsto\!\!\longrightarrow\!\!\longrightarrow\!\!\dashv$

Small Group Discussion

In what ways did you recognize the enemy as you journeyed this week?

_____

_____

_____

_____

When you recognized him were you able to resist? What did you do to fight against his schemes?

_____

_____

_____

_____

How did you replace the lie he tried to sell you?

_____

_____

_____

_____

Bigger is a place of abundance. It comes with more understanding of who God is, more acceptance of who He created us to be and more authority to walk forward in the way He intended us to walk. Take a few minutes to individually reflect back over the past 7 weeks. Then as a group share some of the following answers.

What was the most difficult part of your journey?

_____

_____

_____

_____

_____

In the beginning did you have a hard time believing *bigger*?

_____

_____

_____

_____

When did things click for you (meaning when did the idea of *bigger* start to lead you differently?)

_____

_____

_____

_____

Were there significant people who played key roles in your journey? How has their help changed and inspired you?

_____

_____

_____

_____

How do you know God differently?

_____

_____

_____

_____

How do you see your future differently?

_____

_____

_____

_____

The reality is when we start to understand how big God really is we can't help but dream *bigger*. Living with dreams we can achieve on our own speaks of a little God. We have the attention of the almighty God. He spoke the universe into being and can certainly handle any dreams that might seem just out of our reach.

Ephesians 3:20 says, "He is able to do far more than we could ever ask or imagine." If this verse is true, then think of the *biggest* thing God could do in your life and take it even farther. God wants and will do even more than what you can't imagine right now. He is ready, willing and able, but you have to let Him.

**Our dreams (futures) in our hands are limited;
our dreams in His hands are limitless.**

Week 8—Personal Study Guide

Everything looks different here. Especially you. Especially God. Everything looks different because everything is different. Even when the things surrounding you don't change, the things within you are transformed and that transformation means everything. I am addicted to God's rebuilding process. Learning how perfectly He works in our brokenness has enabled me to look at the broken pieces differently. Even when things around me refuse to budge, His power within me is more than I could imagine. My brokenness may intimidate me, but it doesn't intimidate Him. Experiencing more of Him, because of the broken in my life, has helped me learn to come to the end of myself quicker. The battle to have it all together is waning and I now live with an authentic desire to hand the daily mess over to Him. My desire continues to gain momentum as I move forward.

I don't know how you've met Him in your brokenness, but I'm sure He's blown your mind. He is so delicate with the broken. He is so gentle and tenderhearted. He is patient, giving us piece by piece, only what we can carry, so as not to overwhelm our soul. He walks beside us, steadies our feet and lifts up our arms. He loves talking to us through our rebuilding process. With each broken piece there is a story. With each story there is redemption. With each piece of redemption we receive healing. Healing is addicting. Why settle for less than all He has for us. We are the children of an all-powerful, everlasting, all-consuming Father. He owns the cattle on a thousand hills and everything He has, He offers to us.

Sometimes God heals in the instant, and other times He seems to move at the pace of a turtle. Either way, He values every second of rebuilding. He is all about relationship, all about intimacy and all about connection. Imagine the last trip you took with a friend. Whether it was near or far, spending any amount of time journeying with a friend strengthens your relationship. Uninterrupted time in the car with my husband or my closest friends has produced some of my favorite conversations and memories. We talk, share, laugh, cry, pray, lose track of time, sometimes lose our way, fight to stay awake, eat all kinds of junk food and most definitely rock out to our favorite old school music.

The Father is all about a journey too. He knows the value of uninterrupted time. He loves moving forward together. He knows the value of faith built on the daily miracle of His presence. If you've journeyed to *bigger*, it's likely you now value the miles it took to get here. Those miles, your climb, they represent history with Jesus. They are the stories you tell, the memories you relive and the testimonies you point to first. They will outlast the test of time and they make the broken worth so much more.

Day 1—Bigger Faith

Our faith matters to God. He not only cares we have it; He cares what we do with it. Faith directly affects our ability to continually move forward into *bigger*. In *bigger* we trust God more. We trust His heart and we trust His ability to work on behalf of our future. Take a minute and read the parable Jesus spoke of in Matthew chapter 25:14-30, then answer the following questions.

How many bags of gold did he give to the first servant?_____

The second? _____

The third? _____

What did the first servant do with his bags?

_____

_____

_____

_____

_____

The second?

_____

_____

_____

_____

_____

The third?

_____

_____

_____

_____

_____

When the master returned and the servants brought back his money and their investments, what kind of response did he have?

_____

_____

_____

_____

The master was thrilled to see two of his servants made good use of his money and their time, doubling his initial investment. He blessed them and put them in charge of even more. But to the servant who came back having done nothing was scorned and shamefully sent on his way without anything.

How does the Master's response make you feel?

_____

_____

_____

_____

Write Matthew 25:23b below.

_____

_____

_____

I don't want to live life with my faith buried in a field somewhere. Sometimes the questions running rampant in my head get the best of me: _What if it doesn't work? What if they laugh? What if I look foolish? What if I don't have the right words to say?_

Just like the master gave gold to his servants, God has given each of us a portion of faith. What we do with our portion makes a difference. We cannot bury our faith in a field and expect it to grow. We cannot wrap it up, hide it in the closet, and anticipate it working miracles. Hidden faith will not push us to _bigger_.

John Whimber, founder of the Vineyard Church movement, always said, "Faith is spelled R-I-S-K." In other words, if we want our faith to grow, then we need to do something with it. Faith grows by stepping out. When we step out, we create space for God to step in. When God steps in, He does what we cannot do. In these moments we grow. God is honored when you take the necessary steps to increase your faith. He is committed to helping it grow.

What kind of investment has God given you? Remember an investment can be anything. Maybe God made you good at writing or teaching. Maybe you are a gifted athlete or someone who loves to spend hours upon hours with pre-school children (bless your soul)! No matter who you are God has given you something and what you do with your something makes a difference.

I love to write. Always have. I knew one day I would write a book. However, it did not happen for fifteen years because I wasn't willing to take the risk and put the pen to paper. I wrote safely. I wrote high school lessons, middle school weekend messages, women's prayer experiences, but for the most part, I kept my writing safe and boxed up where I could control it. Taking the risk of putting it out there was one of the scariest things I've ever done. My faith has grown because of it. God showed up (that's what He promises) and He blew my mind (that's also what He promises!)

I wonder if He isn't waiting patiently for you to take a risk with the faith and gift He has given you. Below write one thing you could do to put your investment out there.

_____

_____

_____

Now, spend the remainder of your time today praying into the above step. Pray for courage and opportunity. Pray for wisdom and a *bigger* faith!

Day 2—Bigger Fight

At this point in the journey we can rest easy because we know He is fighting for us. He has already conquered the grave and what He brings us to, He promises to bring us through. I love people with a lot of fight. People who don't give up. Who try over and over again, until they either overcome or they physically can't try anymore. We love going out in our boat. Tubing is one of our favorite family activities. It's even more fun when we get a few teenagers out there with us. Something about being on a tube with a group of students motivates me more than anything. I am determined to hang on longer than they do. Combine that with Dave's drive to make sure we come off and you can bet I've come home with a migraine and back pain a time or two. Those are the moments I remember I am not as young as they are anymore. We boat on Mondays, all summer long. That means on Tuesdays, you can tell how good of a day you had by how high you can lift your arms. Hanging on, battling the water is intense. It activates muscles you didn't know you had. But it's worth every second because victory is sweet.

I'm convinced one of the most hard-core things you can do with your life is make eye contact with Jesus. Locking eyes with Jesus is dangerous because He will call you out. He will invite you to join Him on His mission to bring healing and hope to everyone. Locking eyes with Him is powerful. His eyes are like a magnet, pulling us closer and closer. The longer we look at him, the more we believe. With each step faith grows, but also with each step, danger grows. Danger grows because as we step out, the world around us continues. The waves didn't stop when Peter stepped out of the boat.

Read Matthew 14:22-31.

What happened when Peter realized it was Jesus walking toward them on the water?

_____

_____

_____

_____

_____

Some people read this passage and focus on the lack of faith Peter had, but I read this passage and am instantly drawn to the amount of faith he operated in. It took faith to make eye contact with Jesus out there on the dark, unknown sea. It took courage to call out (the rest of the disciples were hiding in the corner shaking). It took fight to step out of the boat. Who cares if he took a couple of steps and began to sink! I would have freaked out too!

Where in life have you felt like Jesus might be calling you to "come?"

_____

_____

_____

_____

Have you taken any steps to get yourself out of the boat?

_____

_____

_____

_____

What do the waves around you represent?

_____

_____

_____

_____

If you are still inside the boat, what keeps you from stepping? If you're outside of the boat, what has encouraged you to take that initial step?

_____

_____

_____

_____

Fear paralyzes because it keeps us focused on ourselves.
Fight launches us forward, because it keeps us focused on Him.

Write 2 Timothy 1:7 in the space below.

_____

_____

_____

_____

Now write Romans 12:2.

_____

_____

_____

_____

That night on the water, Peter allowed his brave mind to be conformed instead of transformed. When he took his eyes off Jesus, faith turned to fear and his fight to stay on the water overwhelmed him. Had he simply remembered whose presence he was in, those waves wouldn't have looked so threatening. The more I focus on the presence of God with me, the more I am able to overcome. The more I focus on Him, the less I focus on them.

Where are your eyes as you battle in life right now?

_____

_____

_____

_____

Whose presence are you carrying?

_____

_____

_____

What feels impossible in your battle?

_____

_____

_____

Can you remember a time when you gave up in the middle of a battle? What was the outcome? What would you have done differently if you knew then what you know now?

_____

_____

_____

_____

Nothing you are facing is impossible for the Spirit of God living inside of you. Stand up and fight the fight you've been promised to win.

"Even though I walk through the darkest valley, I will fear no evil, for you are with me; your rod and your staff, they comfort me" (Ps. 23:4 NIV).

Day 3—Bigger Future

The natural by-product of allowing God to be *bigger* in all of your life is, He will also become *bigger* in your future. Approaching the future as though we are in control is limiting. In control, we go after things within reach instead of those outside of our grasp. God is not interested in what we can do for Him; He is interested in what we can do with Him. A *bigger* future involves the ability to hold tight to Jesus and loosely to everything else.

I love how the Bible refers to Joseph as a dreamer. I'm a hopeless dreamer. When the God I knew was smaller, my dreams intimidated me. With a *bigger* God, they energize me. We were created to dream big. If our dreams consist of things we can obtain or achieve on our own they aren't really dreams.

The story of Joseph is long so let me summarize it for you here. I would suggest making time to read through it on your own. (Genesis 37, 39, 40, 41)

God gave Joseph a couple of big dreams. In these dreams his older brothers were actually bowing down to him. You can imagine how this made his brothers feel. They already detested Joseph, because he was, by far, his father's favorite. When given the first chance to deal with their dreamy, little brother, they sold him into slavery, sprinkled the blood of a dead animal all over his colorful coat and told their dad he must have been attacked by a wild animal and ripped from limb to limb (*and I thought my brother and I had a rocky relationship growing up!*).

As a slave Joseph was given favor and blessed by God. Potiphar, his master, put him in charge of many things. That is until Potiphar's wife accused Joseph of trying to sleep with her. Joseph was innocent and had done whatever it took to avoid falling victim to his master's wife, but because of her accusations he was thrown into prison.

In prison Joseph was still given favor. The prison guard trusted him and he put Joseph in charge of the daily operations. One day, as Joseph made his rounds he noticed the King's cupbearer and baker were upset. Come to find out, they both had dreams the night before and were struggling with the interpretations. This time, instead of interpreting the dreams his way, Joseph told them God would interpret their dreams.

Two years later, still dreaming in prison, Joseph was summoned to take a shave and a much-needed shower and come stand before Pharaoh. It turns out, Pharaoh had a dream no one knew the meaning of. Joseph's prison mate, who had since then returned to his job in the palace, remembered Joseph. Joseph was brought before Pharaoh. When Pharaoh asked him if he could interpret this disturbing dream, Joseph again responded, "Only God can interpret your dream."

Fast-forward seven years. Because Joseph interpreted Pharaoh's dream correctly, he was put in charge of all of Egypt. During this time there was a famine, which left Joseph's birth family desperate for any type of help they could get. Jacob, Joseph's father, sent his sons into Egypt to go before the Pharaoh for help. As these desperate brothers bowed before the man in charge of all the land, Joseph realized he was looking at his estranged brothers and this scene unfolding before him was the dream God gave him so many years ago.

There is no way Joseph could have ever known all he would go through before the dream God gave him would actually come true. I wonder if he ever gave up on his dream. I wonder if He ever thought he misunderstood. Maybe he even wondered if he was crazy!

Thankfully, God is *bigger* than even the things we give up on. He never gives up. He never lets go.

Do you have a dream in your life you have given up on? If so, what is it?

_____

_____

_____

_____

What caused you to give up on this dream?

_____

_____

_____

Do you think this dream was from God?

_____

_____

_____

Knowing Him the way you do now, do you think you could trust Him with even your biggest dreams?

_____

_____

_____

_____

_____

Through this process I've learned to trust Him. But, I've also learned, things rarely play out as I've planned. He will make our wildest dreams come true, but He will do it His way and in His timing.

What is one thing God has asked you to wait for?

_____

_____

_____

_____

_____

Do you see now why He asked you to wait? How did it His timing work best?

_____

_____

_____

_____

_____

Are you still struggling to believe God has a dream for you? Write Jeremiah 29:11 below.

_____

_____

_____

_____

_____

After you've written it, try writing a prayer to Him. Ask Him to plant a dream in your heart. And then pay attention because He will. He will show up and plant something in your heart, something that will call you into the *bigger*.

_____

_____

_____

_____

_____

_____

_____

_____

_____

Day 4—Bigger for Life

Welcome to *bigger* my friend! I know the journey here hasn't been easy. There have been many days you've wanted to throw in the towel. Many nights you've probably cried yourself to sleep and many winded hours as you've worked to climb your own ladder. But God has been faithful. He always is. He's done a work in you. Together, the two of you (and maybe with the help of a few friends) have rebuilt the crumbled ruins you once saw as useless. Let's talk about how far you've come.

In the beginning of this study, what did the broken pieces surrounding you look like?

_____

_____

_____

When did you start to notice a difference?

_____

_____

_____

What is one of the most valuable things you've heard Jesus whisper to you as you've worked together to rebuild?

_____

_____

_____

_____

For some of us this rebuilding process will take years. Other times it's over in just a few months. What are you feeling about your process of rebuilding and the time it is taking?

_____

_____

_____

Have you reached *bigger*? Are you starting to recognize what it might look like?

_____

_____

_____

_____

One thing I want you to know is *bigger* isn't a one-time thing. God doesn't heal us once then move on to the next person. Healing and rebuilding are parts of a continual process. We live in a broken world, with broken people and unfortunately this means there are layers upon layers of brokenness inside of us. God's plan is to go down deep. He doesn't only intend to heal the branches of your tree. He wants access to the roots because He knows the best thing for a tree, is a healthy set of roots. Healthy roots produce abundant fruit, with little work. Healthy roots are free from day-to-day stress and strain. They are free to work and move forward confidently because they abide in the vine.

You would be limiting the journey if you stopped here. Don't settle for the fruit produced from a one-time journey. Hand that fruit back to your loving Father and ask Him to go deeper. He has so much more in store for you.

The invitation is always for more. I pray you have realized how much you can trust Him with what is broken in your life and in the lives of those you love. How have you seen your trust in Him grow?

_____

_____

_____

_____

What's one thing you will do differently simply because you trust Him more?

_____

_____

_____

_____

Write Zechariah 4:10 below.

_____

_____

_____

_____

When we met Yosselin, God gave us a dream. Trying to figure it out on our own led us to remodeling a bedroom. The small step of remodeling was significant, because it was in that remodel we realized God was _bigger_ than we gave Him credit for. Upon our revelation we took our God-sized dream and handed it back to Him. If this was something God wanted to do, then it was His to do. We agreed to say yes and with every yes, He showed up and showed off. God intended to use our dream to blow our minds.

Each small yes (partnered with the mighty hand of God) built Yosselin a brand new house. God doesn't put a Band-Aid over what's broken, He rebuilds it to be more than we ever imagined possible. Today, Yosselin is living the life of a normal, cancer-free girl. With the story of a God who passionately stepped in and provided for her when she could not provide for herself. God will go to extreme measures to encounter the broken.

This journey is only beginning for you. I believe that. He has so much more to show you. It's more than you could ask or even imagine possible. Really, it is. Think about the biggest things God could for you. The biggest mountain He could climb. The biggest obstacle He could overturn. Now go past it, because what He has for you is even more than that. What He has in store for us, if we will surrender to a life of *bigger,* is more than all the words in this study could even say. Transformation starts today. It's easy to do a study, check the box then put it on the shelf with the rest. It's an entirely different thing to do a study and then let the study become your life. Jesus spends his life in broken places, with broken people. You are in good company to make a new home for yourself where you are radically aware and actively involved in both your brokenness and the brokenness in the world around you. It's always easier to find Jesus if you are committed to being where He is.

Spend the remainder of your time thinking of your next steps. After I've finished a study or a deep time of learning I always like to ask myself the question, "What now?" Now that I've done this, now that I've learned that, what do I do? How does my life change? Why don't you give it a try? Ask yourself the question, "What now?"

_____

_____

_____

_____

_____

_____

_____

_____

_____

_____

_____

Day 5—Challenge Day—Sharing Bigger

The fun thing about the Gospel is it doesn't only change us, it changes the world around us. You are impacted to be an impact. Everywhere you go there is an opportunity for you to make known the love of God. He is everywhere and when you partner with Him the impossible becomes possible.

Today, I want you to come before Jesus on behalf of those around you. I'm sure your family or closest friends have picked up on our little journey. They've noticed your surrender. They've taken note of your obedience. They might even be sensing your *bigger.* Pursuing *bigger* for myself empowers me to speak *bigger* over others. In my experience, God very rarely does something in me and then lets it go at that. Typically, the very thing He has done in me becomes the very thing He then wants to do through me. Because I've been rebuilt, I can now help others rebuild. Because I've fallen in love with the Word of God, I can now help others fall in love with the Word of God. Because I've surrendered my dreams to Him, I can now help others surrender their dreams to Him. Because I've ripped the old, dirty Band-Aids off my own wounds, I can help others do the same. Because you've walked with God through something you too have something to offer those around you. There are always people behind you needing a hand. Think about your day, your community, the people you live life with or even the people you pass on the streets of your town. Part of living a life of continual breakthrough entails not keeping His healing to ourselves. How can you pay it forward and offer someone you know the hope of *bigger?*

As you pay it forward keep in mind, our actions speak louder than our words. Jesus' words were so powerful because He lived them. He didn't just tell his followers to serve, He showed them. It might help by remembering how the people around you helped as you pursued *bigger.* Who were some of those people and what are some of the ways they helped you keep going?

_____

_____

_____

_____

_____

_____

Ephesians 3:14-21 is Paul's final prayer for the Church of Ephesus. Ephesus was a wicked city. They were known for hosting one of the 7 wonders of the world, the famous temple to the Greek goddess, Artemis. The temple and the streets were flooded with immoral goddess prostitutes. People could experience more of the great goddess's power through sexual encounters with her priest and priestesses. Despite the pagan activities Paul successfully shared the Gospel with them and it spread like wildfire. Ephesians, Paul's letter to these new believers, starts with a great reminder of what it means to be adopted into the family of God and it ends with one of my favorite prayers in the entire Bible!

Read this prayer slowly as you close your time today. Make a note of anything God says to you as you read. Meditate on it. Savor it. Digest it. Return to it often. These words are His promise to you. Believe them. Believe Him. Believe bigger.